Old Time Policing

A History of How Policing Was in the
Mid 20th Century

Barrie Davies

authorHOUSE®

AuthorHouse™ UK Ltd.
500 Avebury Boulevard
Central Milton Keynes, MK9 2BE
www.authorhouse.co.uk
Phone: 08001974150

First published by AuthorHouse   9/7/2010

ISBN: 978-1-4520-2388-5 (sc)
ISBN: 978-1-4520-2389-2 (hc)

This book is printed on acid-free paper.

WHAT AM I DOING HERE?

I was sworn in as a Police Constable in 1960 in North Wales after having been a Cadet for a year and, now here I was in June,1966 in London infiltrating , eventually living with, working with and, reporting on a gang of criminals of mixed English and Hungarian races, who were committing crimes in London and the surrounding areas. It was 1963 when I transferred to a North East of England City Police Force and, after some nine months moved to the CID and, was then seconded to the newly formed Regional Crime Squad in April, 1965 It was an outfit that was set up to infiltrate and gain information about major crime and criminals who were spreading themselves about and, taking advantage of the divide lines between police forces. The Crime Squad was there to go over the borders and continue investigations anywhere and investigate and infiltrate the criminal wrong doings, of criminals who were now also starting to use the motorway networks that were being constructed. At this time the Crime Squads were still trying to sell themselves to the local and regional police forces, and show them that it was advancement and, within the police service then advancement was never recognised - "the old methods were always the best!".

Anyway I was in the Crime Squad at an extremely young age, and more than enthusiastic, the adrenalin was flowing freely. I then, by accident, got to know a Hungarian who had moved from London to the north east having met, his by now wife, in London, where she had been working as a prostitute and, they returned to her home area to get out of the heat that was being created by the crime that her now husband was involved in, in the capital and surrounding areas. He and many others from Hungary had fled the country after the 1957 uprising and, many had settled into the community, others had come here to England and continued their criminal activities. They even told me that they were let out of jail to get them out of Hungary. I suppose every country would be delighted to get "rid" of their villains "by deporting them".

The Hungarian had been criminally very active with a gang of the mixture of English and Hungarian villains, they specialised in "smash and grab" raids , their modus operandi being, steal a high powered car, usually a Jaguar, four of them in the car, a driver and three to do the "smash", then drive onto the front of the designated jewellers or furriers, two of them armed with pickaxes would then rush out to put the pickaxes through the shop windows and pull the reinforced glass out and, then the third would throw the displayed jewellery into the boot of the car , display pad by display pad. Once the window was cleared the driver would be at full throttle to speed away from the scene. The more I got to know him, the more information he was giving me. He was trying to establish himself as a decent member of society and, the information he was giving was initially about petty crime in the area which he had chosen to be within with his wife, albeit that she was still prostituting herself, but as he said, "they had to live". A good decent days genuine work never seemed to appeal to them,

A number of his gang related friends would travel north to see him usually when they wanted to get out of the Southern area to avoid capture for whatever recent crimes they had committed. He was obviously a safe house for them in the north of the country. He knew I was a police officer virtually from the first time that I met him and, part of his disguise at being an upstanding citizen was to open a hairdresser shop, but at the same time he was also fully employed during the evenings ferrying other prostitutes about, apart from his wife and, shifting stolen property.

Some months after having met, one of his Hungarian gangland friends came up to see him seemingly to get out of the heat in the kitchen having carried out a smash and grab raid on a furriers that had gone slightly wrong. His friend stayed for a couple of weeks, during which time I had been introduced to him as "Taff", and I was accepted by him as being just a member of the local criminal fraternity and a mate of his mate. They both decided to leave the north and return to the London area as money was tight and, a return to London was needed to get their ill-gotten gains,. from where ever and by whatever means they could.

A day went past after they had left and , the phone rang in the crime squad office and, Marjory the secretary put it through to my desk, telling me that it was Joe on the line wanting to speak to me, obviously the Boss and the squad were aware of what was going on with regard to the nurturing of my gaining information from him. Following the initial "How are you", he went on to tell me that the gang were doing numerous smash and grab raids throughout London and the surrounding areas and, they had asked him to be the driver. He then went on to tell me that if I went down there I could join them and get the information back to get them locked up. The acceptance value for me was a question of me being accepted by the gang and that question had to be asked and, he then told me that his friend who had stayed with him had already spoken about me when they had been together with others and that he didn't think there would be any problem with regard to acceptance.

What was in it for him contacting me and being a "grass"?. I suppose it was the thought of being on the right side for once, trying to prove himself as being a citizen who should stay in the UK by co-operating with the police (despite his wife's build up of clients in the north east) and, if he wasn't constantly in touch with his old gang mates he would always be suspected of being the one who exposed them. There was also a plus to it for him, that being , information gratitude in the name of pounds, shillings and pence, which was paid following information given whereby there was an arrest and conviction, that he received those pounds shillings and pence as "Informant's pay off.".

All things considered, I was off to the big City with the permission of the Crime Squad Regional Co-ordinator, but without guarantee of safety or prosecution as "Agent Provocateur" , in fact it was never mentioned. The name of the game was to put as many villains away as possible, no matter how just and establish the Crime Squad and justify its existence.

There was no question of the "Agent Provocateur" factor, because no-one suggested, induced, encouraged or provoked any of the members of this gang to do anything required to be considered a criminal target, they would have done anything for monetary profit, as such they just considered it collectively and it was a joint decision by them after having thoroughly discussed and planned any job they were about to undertake. They were professional in every regard concerning their crimes committed. It was a mixture of English and Hungarian criminal activity for their gain without any thought towards their victims and the effect of their deeds on society as a whole, so why not make and use every effort to incarcerate them and deport them if circumstances allowed.

I was now on the train to London, the big City, I'd only been there once before for a day, I was going to the unknown and, into the unknown. I arrived at Kings Cross and sure enough Joe was there and, when we met his welcome was such as a long lost friends. He guided me to a nearby pub where he ordered the drinks, which I was pleased about , because my initial allowance was fifty pounds and, that was to pay for accommodation and eat, I was then to liaise with the "Flying Squad" at Scotland Yard who would give me every backing that I wanted and, react on any information given to them. That was soon to be proved to be untrue.

We were in the pub when suddenly Joe was totally surprised or so he said, that a number of his gang mates came in, he then introduced me as "Taff". I seemed to be accepted and, as conversation continued , from what Joe had been telling them, together with his mate who had been staying with him, I was, it seemed accepted as an escapee from Walton prison in Liverpool. It was then eventually accepted that I "was up for anything". That acceptance, didn't happen over night, but did after a number of further gatherings.

I was in on the act, every job was researched and carried our to perfection. It was a matter of finding a hit, doing the job, and getting rid of the proceeds and spending the money. It was my job to act with them and, pass the information back to the Flying Squad at Scotland Yard, which I did, but the problem was that those officers I had been liaising with could not be relied upon, so I learned in the months to come, that some of my so called colleagues in the Flying Squad were as much involved in criminal activities as the gang members that I was amongst.

My initiation into actively taking part in a smash and grab raid was on a clothing shop in Seven Sisters Road in North London. The job was set up by a Brian Scrivens, Brian, as it eventually transpired was a prison escapee after doing two years of a six year sentence for armed robbery. He had been on the run for two years and was living in the Fulham area with quite a stunning female, but had kept his freedom by virtue of paying a detective in Fulham a weekly rent for that freedom, because he had previously identified him and done nothing about it, other than charge him rent for that freedom. Sadly that was to be my continued experience of certain officers of the Metropolitan Police, it was a case of "who could I trust?". Scrivens was a man who could mix in any circle, he was good looking and, a total charmer, but just prior to going on any job he went into his shell, his mind was on nothing but the "Deed to be Done".

Brian Johnson, was another member of the selected team, and he was yet another escapee having been on the run for two years out of a four year sentence for armed robbery.

The other three enlisted to do the job, was me, Joe and, Legos Trestyen, who it was said had left Hungary after being let out after being incarcerated for murder, but the truth of that I couldn't establish, but nevertheless I could imagine it as being a truthful statement because of his attitude and behaviour, which was non-caring towards anyone or any situation.

The Seven Sisters Road job was unusual in respect of there being five of us, as there was only four usually on any job, but the job was being done because we wanted kitting out, so why pay for it, just "nick it". That was the attitude and the mode of life.

The usual plan was obviously that the driver would remain in the car when the others got out and, either one or two would attack the window and, the remainder ,whether it be one or two, would remain on the pavement to dispel any "crime watch do-gooders" as they were termed, who wished and wanted a crime free life, which from time immemorial has proved to be impossible".

On this job the car had been nicked, it was a Jaguar with plenty of go, which had been left in a car park for four or five days after being nicked, so for that period of time it hadn't been sussed , because checks had been made on it during its placement and it was clear it was free for use. It had been decided that it was going to be an early morning job on the clothiers. Those among the gang were totally fearless , but obviously protective of their liberty and did picked up the car, circled the property to see that all was clear, which it was, It was then a case of storming in, stopping outside the property, in with the pickaxes, load the suits shirts and whatever into the car, boot or wherever and, of to go.

It was a successful getaway to a period of wearing goods, (very good) quality gear, to go wherever you wished at the expense of the retailer or could it be the insurance company with a bit added onto the claim?.

This was a testing time, I had got the confidence of those members of the gang, I knew what they were about, I'd identified them and, the question was where do we go from here?. They were obviously a serious gang of both English and Hungarian participants and, non could be trusted .

The questions had to be answered, should they be arrested for this job, on the job, or let go to commit further crime. The answer was that if they were "copped" for this one, how would it look?, They would be looking for someone who had "spilt the beans". I could have been singled out having been on the first job, they could also have " eye balled" Joe, because they had all trusted each other and stayed free on previous jobs. The decision was to leave well alone and to let me and those involved walk around in the designer gear of that era, which we did.

The development of my relationship with the gang I was involved with and, the engagement I had with the Flying Squad had to be judged and, truth be known I trusted the villains more than the Flying Squad. Isn't that sad?, but that was a matter of fact. Surely if a youngster from Yorkshire, ex-North Wales, a simpleton who had trespassed into the Metropolitan Flying Squad domain, could suss them out, and also what was their occasion of splendour, shouldn't the Met. Police have sussed them out before?.

My involvement with the gang continued for the next six months , but it's surely better to know how it all started as a career within a small police force in North Wales - so, "I'LL TELL YOU HOW IT STARTED!".

A Probationary Police Experience AS IT WAS IN 1958!. It was a winters day and I was off work after having been injured playing football. , I had left grammar school and started to work at a chemical factory as an apprentice draftsman, which was not far from the market town where I lived in North Wales, I hated it. To become a draftsman you had to go through the engineering side first and learn the basics. That was part of the process of learning and could be accepted, but what could not be accepted was the filth that you were breathing in within and without the factory, health and safety just didn't exist. It was on January 7th 1958 that I read in the local paper that the local constabulary were to recruit two cadets between the ages of 18years and nineteen years, nineteen years being the age that one could become a fully fledged constable, provided you were 6 feet tall, of good physique, fully fit and above all, a person of integrity and average intelligence. I seemed to fit the bill (to coin a phrase) and I so happened to be passing the constabularies headquarters, so it seemed appropriate to call in and inquire, which I did.

The force had an establishment of one hundred and twenty five men and five women officers, and they were responsible for policing a large area, both urban and rural. The Chief Constable was an Oxford graduate and a former Welsh rugby international.

The headquarters was adjacent to the divisional headquarters in a relatively small sandstone building, which housed offices, a canteen and sufficient cells for transgressors of the law. On entering the headquarters entrance I was met by a sergeant who was extremely smart and to the point, "Yes young man what can I do for you?". I explained to him that I had seen the advert in the local paper regarding the recruitment of cadets and that I wanted to apply, to which he replied, "We are interviewing certain young men now, do you wish to stay to be interviewed?". It came as a bit of a shock, but my reply was "Yes".

The interview was before the Chief Constable, his Deputy and the Sergeant who had met me at the door. The interview started by me being asked if I spoke the Welsh language, to which I replied "Yes". The rest of the interview was about my sporting prowess, education and, the obtaining of two references before it being confirmed that I was to be appointed.

Some ten days later I received notification that my appointment was confirmed. I handed in my resignation at the chemical factory and, I was then ready for the start of twenty five years of upholding the law. I was kitted out with uniform and started the learning process within the legal system, as it was then in 1958 and, continued to so learn at the University of Life until my retirement some twenty five years later.

I was posted to the divisional headquarters and found myself in the admin office to basically experience the general running of the division. One of the tasks set me was recording by ledger the crime statistics for each area within the division and, it was remarkable to see the crime scene from area to area. One quite extensive rural area was policed by a Sergeant and a Constable and, the crime committed within that area during the year was one, that was detected so they had a one hundred percent detection rate. The crime committed was suicide and therefore could not go undetected. (Suicide at that time being a criminal offense.)

It wasn't long before I was let out on the public accompanied by an experienced officer, during which time I had my first arrest, that being a drunk that I saw stealing a bottle whisky from a shop by taking it off the shelf and walking out without paying. By chance I was at the time looking through the window of the shop and arrested him when he came out. He duly appeared before the court and was sentenced to four weeks in prison. It was my first claim to fame by upholding the law which resulted in a sub-headline in the local press which read "Alert cadet spotted him.".

Time progressed and my nineteenth birthday arrived and I was duly appointed a Constable of her Majesties Constabulary and was on my way to a police training center in South Wales for a period of twelve weeks. It was a grueling task with lectures, drill, character and fitness building and two days break every four weeks and, most of that time was taken up by traveling to and from home.

TRAINING

Training was arduous, but it had its advantages by being taught how to react as an individual and together with others and above all it was character building. It also enabled one to make friends with other recruits from all over the south of England and the whole of Wales. It also had its laughs, its serious side and the unexpected. The laughs came naturally, the serious side was the learning and the development of character and, the unexpected in my case came about by the process of nature.

If we were in the training center over the week end we were allowed out of base on the Saturday evening, restricted to a curfew of eleven p.m. By far the majority of us on the Saturday evening headed for the Palaise de Dance in the center of town, about fifteen minutes walk away from the center. It was an all male decent on the dance hall - there being no females at the center - and the object of the exercise was to eye-up the local talent, drink until ten p.m. (the then drinking up time) and pick up a local lass in good time to say good night and meet the curfew time.

There were three courses at the center at anyone time and therefore one course was leaving every month and, on the Friday prior to the course finishing there was a passing out parade, a cross-country run and a dance during the evening which included all students. It was the Saturday prior to my first month at the center when with others I went to the Palais de Dance, we danced, drank and it was there that I met this auburn haired young lady and it was arranged that I would walk her home. I asked her where she lived and she then told me that she lived in the Instructor's houses which were above the center, she then went on to tell me that her father was one of the drill instructors, to which I gulped - they were like Gods. She saw my reaction and she comforted and reassured me and, we continued to walk towards her home. She suggested that we went into the outhouse at the rear of the house, which we did and the scene became quite passionate. The coal house was at the rear of the outhouse, the location of which I didn't know, but was soon to find out when the door opened and, standing there with a coal shovel in his hand was one of the drill sergeants. There were no good byes, I grabbed my discarded attire and moved at some considerable speed out of the outhouse and away with the resounding shout in my ear, "I'll get you. You bastard.".

The following Monday arrived and I was present on parade first thing in the morning smartly dressed and shining bright, needless to say the drill sergeant was the one and same that had been hurling abuse at me on the previous Friday night when I was fleeing his outhouse without saying a final farewell to his daughter. The Inspector taking the parade past me followed by the drill sergeant, who had the peak of his cap touching his nose and causing him to squint. He leaned towards me and whispered in my ear "I will f----ing well get you sonny boy, your turn is coming.". I stood there in total trepidation and wondering what the week would bring.

Friday arrived, the passing out parade went without incident and in the afternoon the cross-country started on time. The course was one of five or six miles and, being pretty adept at long distance running and also wanting to win the race and get an early shower to prepare for the evening dance, I shot ahead and was way in front of the other ninety to a hundred participants. When I arrived at the finishing line, which was the gate to the center, I was met by two "Drill Pigs" who doubled up as P.E. Instructors, one of whom was the coal shovel monster who had thrown abuse at me on the previous Saturday and threatened me on the following Monday.

He shouted me over, "Get your body here. You couldn't get round that quick. You're a f---ing cheat, run it again, Go-Go-Go and report to me when you get back". I had no option, but to carry on running. On my eventual return to the center there was no-one to meet me, so I went in search, thinking all the while that he should have known that I could run pretty quick because he had seen me at full gallop on the previous Saturday night. I searched all evening for him, to no avail and in consequence missed the dance much to the amusement of the rest of the billet when they returned after the dance, telling me that the auburn haired young lady had attended in all her glory, obviously at the invite of her father.

The course came to an end without any more reprisals, the report was good and, I returned to my force, to the same market town in North Wales for a period of two years probation.

LET LOOSE ON THE PUBLIC

The regime was pretty strict and the attendance for duty was to work three shifts on a weekly basis - 6a.m. to 2p.m., 2p.m. to 10p.m. and, 10p.m. until 6a.m. The order of dress was a dog-collared uniform, helmet, boots, raincoat, overcoat, whistle and cape. There were no personal radios, but the radios for the vehicles had just arrived and had just been fitted. The first vehicle to be fitted was shown to the Chief Constable outside the police garage, and I had the privilege of being present where the vehicle was parked below the control room, everyone was in awe of being able to speak from the vehicle to the control room, little was it realized that the county was mountainous and therefore if the vehicle was in the shadow area of a mountain or cliffs then there was no contact. One was out on patrol with, for protection, a whistle, a truncheon and a torch. For the first two weeks of duty as a probationer you were assigned to an experienced officer for guidance before being let out alone on the public.

My two weeks were completed when I received notification that I was being transferred from "A" Division to "B" Division, to a town with a bay on the North Wales Coast and the headquarters of the division, the country side to police was vast, urban and rural. The structure of command was a Superintendent, two Inspectors (one of which was a Detective Inspector), five Sergeants and the rest were Constables.

The colleagues were great pals, hardworking and genuine, the back up from senior ranks was questionable because they were never about when wanted. One in particular comes to mind, Llew Roberts, who was the typical robust Sergeant, wearing his dog collar uniform fitted to his rotund mid-drift and always with his pacing stick to hand

and displaying his numerous military medal bands on his chest. On night duty after the customary parade, Llew would summon back one of the shift to take him home , which was some three miles from the H.Q., for him to spend the night in slumber and, with the orders for him to be collected at 5.30a.m. to discharge the night shift.

It didn't always work out as planned by Llew, because there is no way in which events can be predicted. If Llew had a lift home to slumber he was taken in the Divisional vehicle, which was a Bedford Bullnose van that had been driven by every member of the division and was the only general vehicle available (there were only three other vehicles in the division, a C.I.D. Morris Minor van and two Vauxhall Crestas and, that was to cover the whole of the vast acreage of the division), the Bedford van had a column change of three gears and all the gates dividing the gears were non-existent and the engine had no energy. The vehicle was ready for the scrap heap, but never seamed to reach there.

The area was a place where many elderly people went to retire and in consequence you soon became versed in dealing with sudden deaths when one acted as the Coroner's Officer. The deceased were always treated with the greatest of respect and, on one glorious summer afternoon I was summonsed by Llew Roberts to attend at a sudden death at a home not far from the police station. Together with the Sergeant I climbed the hill to the address where the death had occurred and on the way there he told me that he knew the family and had for a time some years previous lived with them. It transpired that the elderly gent had collapsed and died in the kitchen while eating his dinner. He had been ill for some time and had a bed in a down stairs room and my instructions were to take him from the kitchen along a corridor to his bedroom and prepare him by removing his clothing and placing him on his bed to await the undertaker while the Sergeant comforted the family and had a cup of tea.

It was extremely hot and the sweat poured out of me as I struggled to carry out the instructions without one iota of help. The task was completed and the Sergeant appeared looking extremely sad while consoling the family, only to say to me,"What are you sweating for lad?". There was no answer to that except to get on with the task and prepare the sudden death report.

The reward came at a later date when I was standing in the centre of the town on duty when the undertaker drove past and beckoned me over to him and handed to me a one pound note as a recompense for having called him to deal with the families bereavement. I refused the gift, but was quickly reassured by the undertaker that it had been a practiced custom for many years that the undertaker recompensed the officer who had requested their services, so so-be it it wasn't for me to change a long standing custom especially when the police salary was a pittance which was some twelve pounds a fortnight which included rent, torch and boot allowance.

TORCHY AND THE MORTUARY

It was the duty of the officer on a certain beat at night to check the mortuary for any property that may have been left there. The mortuary was in the center of the town at the far end of a car park where there was no lighting. On the particular night in question the officer on the beat was "Torchy" and it was therefore his duty to collect the keys to the mortuary from the telephone room prior to going out on his beat, which he did.

"Torchy" was so called because he was petrified of the dark. In stature he was six foot four inches tall and as thin as a lat and, on nights he always paraded for duty with his six cell battery torch with which he would walk down the center of the roads and alleyways shining from side to side.

This particular night I was detailed to man the telephones, which was the old plug in system and considered antiquated in those days and, it was my duty to hand the keys to the officer covering the mortuary beat and, on request I duly handed "Torchy" the mortuary keys. During the early hours of the morning, one of the constables, Ken Cunningham came into the telephone room and requested the spare set of keys for the mortuary saying that "Torchy" had mislaid the other set, so I naturally gave them to him knowing that an account for both sets would have to be made at a future time.

Ken Cunningham was a ginger haired robust officer with some eighteen years experience or thereabouts and certainly one for having a joke.

At this time there were no refrigerators in the mortuary, just slabs and white plastic sheets which had usually seen better times.

It so happened that Cunningham had gone to the mortuary before "Torchy" and in the dark laid on the slab and placed one of the white plastic sheets over himself. He laid there motionless until "Torchy" unlocked the door of the mortuary, put the light on and went to check the property book. At that time, still covered by the plastic sheet, Cunningham slowly sat up, putting the fear of death literally into "Torchy".

I, not knowing what had happened, saw "Torchy" running into the telephone room, carrying his helmet and his torch and with his overcoat wide open. He said nothing, but rushed to the toilet where it could be heard that he was being violently sick.

Shortly following this episode Cunningham came into the telephone room also carrying his helmet and holding his head saying "That bloody "Torchy crusted me.". I transpired that as Cunningham was rising on the slab, covered by the white sheet, "Torchy" hit him with his torch right across the forehead and departed like a bat out of hell, leaving the light on and the mortuary door wide open.

Cunningham was left to fend for himself and treat his wounds when he came around after being laid out by "Torchy" and, left to dwell on the thoughts that practical jokes can sometimes be painful.

CHECKING THE QUARRY

Surrounding towns and villages rarely had patrols after 10p.m. until 6a.m. unless there was anything special occurring and therefore it was up to the divisional headquarters to police them using the dilapidated column change three gear Bedford van. You were lucky that the sliding doors remained attached to the body as you closed them, you were lucky if there was any charge in the battery, you were certainly lucky to find the gears and you were certainly lucky to be able to see by the use of the virtually non-existent headlamps.

There were certain properties that had to be checked in the surrounding areas and one such property was an explosive store at a quarry. The quarry was right on the sea front some way below the main North Wales `A` road. It's approach was an unlit two lane tarmac carriageway for some thirty yards descending to a single gravel covered carriageway. The descent was steep and led firstly to a one train track level crossing, beyond the crossing the road continued to wind for some distance underneath a high rock face and eventually led to a flat rock surface which was some thirty yards in length by approximately twenty yards in width and on the sea side of the plateau was a shear drop to the sea of some fifty feet or more. The sea could always be heard beating up against the rocks as a continuous reminder of the danger created by the edge and beyond and, on a stormy winters night the sound of the sea was deafening and frightening. The concrete explosives store was at the far end of the plateau on the land side.

It was my shifts turn for night duty and together with a fellow officer named Nigel I was designated to checking the properties and patrolling the surrounding towns and villages, needless to say in the Bedford van, After having managed to start the vehicle at approximately 10.30p.m. we set off to examine properties and patrol the areas to the west of the town, then working our way south and eventually to the east. When on this patrol you took your packing up with you and then would stop at a convenient place and time to devour whatever the landlady had packed you up with and have a cup of tea out of your flask.

We had reached the area to the east of the town and stopped to have our pack up, we couldn't stop for long and really didn't want to, because there was no heating in the vehicle and we couldn't have the light on because of the use of the battery and the trepidation that if we switched the engine off we wouldn't get the van started again.

At this time there had been a number of safe-break-ins in the Liverpool and North Wales area and explosive stores had also been targeted and broken into at various places, so it was imperative that we checked the quarry explosives store.

We set off again on this dark windy cold night and reached the turn off leading to the quarry. I was driving, taking the descent carefully, because the brakes were not too good and in particular the handbrake was almost ineffective, it was a case of finding and using the low gears. We eventually made the plateau where it was pitch black, the noise of the sea battering the rocks below was deafening and we couldn't see much in front of us because of the lights of the vehicle being so poor.

We were half way across the plateau when we saw a vehicle near to the concrete store, at least it appeared to be a vehicle from what we could see. Nigel must have seen it at the same time as me, but spoke before me, "Bloody hell, I haven't seen a car down here before!". The adrenaline started to flow and I'm sure that the heart beats could have been heard above the noise of the sea. We were then very close to the vehicle and seemed to both see a figure within the dim lights of the Bedford at the same time. I said, "Jesus, we've got bloody company!". By this time Nigel had his truncheon in one hand and his torch in the other, it went without saying that the whistle was of no use.

I pulled the vehicle to a stop and we both immediately saw that there were three males with the car. I pulled the van door to open, it groaned with the usual squeaks and, force eventually opened it. Nigel's door when he pulled it opened so far and refused the remainder of the journey, which caused him to have to squeeze his was out.

We could now easily see the three men as I had left the vans engine running with the lights as full on as they could be. We were both shouting at the men to stay still, but our words could hardly be heard, if at all, because of the waves hitting the rocks. One of the three ran at me and with my truncheon to hand I instinctively swung out and hit him across the head which caused him to stop and, in doing so, receive another crack which floored him. With the heart continuing to race and the wonder of what was going to happen next the scene changed somewhat when the other two made it known that they were at that time accepting that they had been caught. They both went to their partner in crime and found that he was not conscious but breathing.

They had been disturbed right in the middle of the act of breaking into the store by setting explosives to detonate to be able to get into the store.

I went to the van, which was only a few feet away, while Nigel stood over the perpetrators with his truncheon and torch at the ready to do a "Torchy".

The van, albeit in the condition it was, had been fitted with a radio, but it didn't work and wouldn't have done anyway because of the cliff face. There was no option therefore other than to load the van with the prisoners and cart them to the police station and get medical help for the injured one, who by this time was moaning, but still prostrate.

Knowing that the radio was useless and no help was on hand I went to Nigel and said, "Let's get the buggars in the van!", to which he replied in his broad welsh accent, "Shall we caution them now?". He was obviously thinking about his training and doing things by the book. I couldn't believe my ears and just said, "One can't hear you and the sea won't let the other two hear you, so get them in the van."

It was with shouts to the two conscious prisoners to pick their mate up and put him in the van, which was done with the necessary gesticulation so that they could understand despite the fierceness of the noise of the sea. That they duly picked there counter part up and placed him into the back of the van and got in themselves with Nigel following them. I closed the back doors of the van, but they were not able to be locked because the lock simply didn't work.

I got into the van with the engine still running and put the vehicle into first gear to pull away and turn the vehicle to face the graveled winding hill to exit the dark hole that we were in. When I got into the vehicle the wind was blowing at speed through the passenger door which Nigel had been unable to close and through the driving side door. I managed to close the driver's door which echoed the usual noises,creaking as it closed. After having turned half way to face the hill, which I couldn't see at that point because of the poor lights of the vehicle, I stopped to put the vehicle into reverse to complete the full turn. It was hell to find the reverse gear, but eventually I managed it, now it was a repeat performance trying to find the first gear which I eventually did and set off in the direction of the gravel surfaced winding single track hill.

The plan was to get the vehicle into second gear and as much momentum as possible to have a good start on the ascent. The start of the incline appeared in the dim headlights, but the vehicle was moving at snails pace because of there being five persons in the vehicle. I started up the hill with the van painfully struggling but managing to make the first bend, just!. At the beginning of the bend the only choice I had was to try and put the vehicle into first gear to get further momentum. I hit the clutch which had to be completely depressed before it engaged and then pushed the column gear change lever into neutral and with the gears grinding I was now faced with finding first gear. Frantically, and with a great deal of gear box grating, which could be heard above the noise of the wind and the sea, I managed to engage first gear. The vehicle moved forward, perilously slowly. I knew it wasn't going to make the climb with so many bodies in it. I shouted to those in the back that they were going to have to get out and push. I had my right hand on the steering wheel my right foot to the floor on the accelerator and my left hand on the handbrake. The vehicle was hardly moving on the gravel.

Nigel and the two fit prisoners scrambled out of the rear doors after having opened them from the inside and, causing me to think that it was a good job that the lock didn't work, because I could not have left the driving seat as the brakes just would not have held the vehicle. The reduction of weight and the pushing stared to assist our climb albeit very slowly. To any onlooker knowing the circumstances it would have been an episode from the "Keystone Cops".

The climb seemed to take for ever with the perpetual fear of the van stopping, the brakes being unable to hold it and it slipping back on the gravel to where we had come from and possibly an early bath, were the thoughts going threw my mind.

In the dim lights I saw the Tarmac roadway and wanted to shout with delight, but there was still work to be done to reach it. We reached the Tarmac, but our journey to safety was not complete until we reached the `A` road to take us down hill to the headquarters, which with continued determination we did.

I stopped the van on the most level piece of road that showed up in the light that we had. Nigel and the two prisoners were knackered and, the prisoners could have just scampered, but they hardly had the strength to get back into the van never mind run away and their mate was still in no condition to go with them.

With everyone in the vehicle I drove off, with my stomach feeling less sick and my heart lifted, towards the police station. We had to pass the hospital on the way, but the injuries to the prisoner did not seem to be life threatening and if we had have stopped for him to receive treatment there was no officer to stay with him, so it was a `B` line for the Police Station.

On our arrival I stopped the vehicle, thankful to get out, and got the able bodied prisoners to assist their partner in crime into the charge room, only to find that there was no Sergeant present because the duty Sergeant was Llew Roberts and he was in a state of slumber at his home abode and to be collected at 5.30a.m. His sleep was disturbed by a telephone call to his home when the circumstances of the arrest were briefly told to him and, for him to be told that there was no-one available to pick him up because one of the prisoners had to be taken to hospital and all officers were fully engaged. It didn't go down too well with Llew who had to use his own car to return to duty with the mood of a man who had been awakened too early from his slumber.

The injured prisoner was treated at the hospital and remained in under observations for the rest of the day and then returned to the Police Station to be jointly charged with attempting to break into the explosives store and being in possession of explosives. They were all from Liverpool and eventually admitted being jointly responsible for the series of safe breakings in the Liverpool and North Wales area and also the breaking into other explosive stores. They were remanded in custody to be committed to Quarter Sessions.

In those days all the evidence was heard before the Magistrates and typed out by their Clerk for the prisoners to be committed, they were duly committed.

At the committal all three pleaded guilty and the accused who had wanted to use violence was sentenced to eight years imprisonment and leniency was shown to the other two for assisting, after being arrested, as they did, and they were sentenced to six years imprisonment.

Nigel and I were both commended by the Judge on the arrest and the detection of the crimes, and the Judge went on to say that he hoped the condition of the Bedford van would be brought to the attention of an appropriate person - it never was to my knowledge!.

THE EISTEDDFOD - THE BEST PERFORMANCE

In the approximate center of the picturesque county is a town which has beautiful scenery with mountains all the way around, a fast flowing river over a rocky bed, and magnificent views and a canal with horse drawn boats for the pleasure of the public. Annually there is held an International Eisteddfod with as many as eighty or ninety different countries participating and concerts each evening by famous artists. Those participating in the song and dance and those supporting are in national dress, making the scene even more spectacular. This carries on for a week ending with a final concert by an internationally famous artist.

The increase in the number of persons in the town during the week is quite phenomenal and, the behaviour of the people is usually exceptionally good causing there to be an extremely friendly atmosphere with a total friendship between nations. Nevertheless the area required to be policed and called for an increase in the number of officers to police the area and officers were drafted into the town from all corners of the county.

Where I was stationed was some fifty miles away and I was one of three officers seconded to the Eisteddfod town for the week to patrol between mid-day and mid-night. It wasn't a case of staying overnight during that week because there were no hotel or guest house vacancies and neither was there the finance to cover the cost, or so we were told. There was also no overtime payment, but merely some time off in lieu of the extra hours worked, if you were lucky enough ever to get them. Needless to say the journey to and from my station to the Eisteddfod town was a laborious journey in the Divisional Bedford van, which called for an early start to be sure of getting there by mid-day. We had uneventful journey's in both directions during the week other than on the final Sunday night, the journey's prior to that however did cause the rump to suffer after being sat on the wooden lath seats in the vehicle, the anxiety of whether or not we would arrive on time and having the wax in our ears loosened by the noise of the van's engine and the rattles of the body work and parts.

It was the final return journey when the problems arose. The final concert went on and on and finished around mid-night, we were pleased that the audience enjoyed the artist of world renown, but there were some of us who wanted to get home. We eventually finished at one in the morning or thereabouts at the Eisteddfod showground and then had to make our way , some considerable way back to the Police Station, to be discharged and sentenced to the journey back to our divisional headquarters in the Bedford van.

The journey commenced with the usual disarray of happenings within the vehicle and we made our way out of the town by instinct with the help of a full moon supplementing the van's headlights. The police sign on the vehicle was above the windscreen and we daren't put that on for fear of the battery packing up. The Pass that we had to traverse was an extended horseshoe in shape and extremely steep, but it had to be traversed to get to the road to lead us home. We managed the Pass - Just!. After having traveled a couple of miles and eventually reaching third gear there was nothing left in the engine and we just stopped, to be fair to the engine, we didn't know whether or not it was that or the clutch.

After having stopped in no-mans land, on the top of a mountain, with a radio in the vehicle which chose not to work at any time, but looked good, we were stranded, as luck would have it a car passed which we were able to stop and gain a lift to the nearest farm house which must have been a mile to a mile an a half away to summons help. I was designated to beckon help and travel to the nearest farm for assistance, when we pulled up at the nearest farm house I was pleased to see that they had telephone lines. I knocked on the door, there was a dog barking but there was no reply, I tried the door and found that it was not locked, the dog was still barking but there was still no response from the occupants. I opened the door and found it to be quite bright from the moonlight, there was no-one downstairs and I made my way upstairs where all the doors were open. I had no torch or other light than that from the moon to assist me and, it was with a sudden jolt that I was brought to a halt in a Half Nelson. I thought that my head was going to be screwed off, suddenly the farmer seemed to realize that he was restraining a uniformed "copper", and he released his grip, much to my relief.

Thankfully the farmer and his wife, three children and the dog, were completely understanding of our plight, and were only too pleased to assist us using their telephone to contact the headquarters for transport to be sent out to us. They were told at headquarters that I would stay where I was to be collected after the other two stranded with the van and, in the meantime I was treated to a cup of tea and a sandwich which was extremely welcome, albeit in the middle of the night. The good Samaritan driver wanted to be on his way after being delayed, so I bid him farewell and thanked him for his services. I was met eventually by the others and traveled back to the divisional headquarters, in state, in one of the new patrol cars which had a radio that did work.

During the week I had been reunited with Phil Roberts, a Constable who was stationed at my previous division. Phil was a man mountain of a man, a gentle giant, who was about thirty years of age and, always handy to have around when there was any kind of problem. Prior to joining the police force he had been brought up and worked on a farm where the Welsh language was predominant, albeit that his spoken English was good with a broad welsh accent, his written English left a lot to be desired and caused him problems when writing reports.

I was able to help Phil with his reports and he was always extremely grateful, but I wasn't about all the while and in consequence some of his reports were submitted without correction. The reports would inevitably land on the desk of the Chief Inspector who would have Phil called in to ridicule him. The Chief Inspector was a big man with a large unkempt moustache and a mid-rift of similar proportion and he so happened to be the senior officer during the week.

Refreshments were provided for officers during their meal break in the Magistrates Court which was above the police station and, it was on a beautiful summers day, when Phil and I went in for refreshments at the same time. Both of us were boiling hot in our dog collared uniforms and went to a serving table to collect our meals which were salads, the same as everyone else was having because there was no choice. We took our seats next to each other and placed our meals before us on the court table. The person at the head of the table was non other than the Chief Inspector, He was sitting in the Clerk to the Court's chair busily talking to a civilian sitting to his left and at the same time gorging his salad causing salad cream to drip from his moustache and also causing his belly to extend beyond the edge of the table. We had started to eat our meals when Phil nudged me and leaned towards me and whispered in my ear "Look at that bloody caterpillar on the fat bastards lettuce.". I looked towards the Chief Inspector's plate and saw this green and yellow caterpillar wriggling about on his lettuce. The Chief Inspector continued his gorging and talking and, I leaned towards Phil and whispered in his ear, "Tell him!", to which Phil replied in his broad welsh accent, "Bugger him!". The next two fork-fulls' of lettuce were stuffed into his mouth narrowly missing the caterpillar but the third fork-full lifted the caterpillar together with lettuce and other salad ingredients into his mouth and he started to chew when Phil turned towards the Chief Inspector and said with a deep welsh lilt, "Ey Sir, you've just eaten a bloody caterpillar, it was green and yellow.".

The Chief Inspector looked directly at Phil and didn't know whether to throw up or swallow. He tried to say something and at the same time gulped and that was the end of the caterpillar. He swung his bulk out of his chair and headed for the toilets and, as he went through the courtroom doors Phil burst into a raucous contagious laugh saying, "That serves the fat bastard right.". The contagious laugh caused others of us present to also burst out laughing at the same time as we were quickly finishing our meals to get out before he returned. That was some way to get his own back after having had his reports thrown back at him.

When we returned to our beats it was still boiling hot and we couldn't stop laughing at having seen the Chief Inspector baulking. Our beats were adjacent on the river bridge in the centre of the town. The town was packed and the atmosphere was wonderfully friendly and the cafes and hostelries were full and there was a hotdog van at the end of the bridge on my side which was manned by two females and doing a rip-roaring trade.

As dusk was falling I was approached by a man and wife who had just got a hot-dog and the man said to me, "Some thing's not right with those two in there!" - indicating towards the van. I asked him, "Why?" to which he said, "We're both sure that they're men dressed up, we're not eating our hot-dogs!". Phil was at that time on the opposite side of the bridge and I beckoned him over and, he walked across still with a big smirk on his face, obviously still thinking of the caterpillar in the salad. I repeated to him what had been said to me and he said, "Let's go and have a look."

I was of the understanding that they must have had Local Authority permission to park where they were and in consequence trading authentically, but that proved not to be the case. Phil turned to me and said, "They're bloody well right, look at the wigs and (pointing to one of them) his tits are sagging.". We both walked to the side door of the van and opened it, to which one of them said, "We'll be with you in a minute." They were extremely busy and selling hot dogs as if they were going out of fashion. Phil said, "We haven't got a minute!". He reached forward saying to the people near to the serving hatch, "Move back please they're closing.". With that he closed the hatch and, at the same time the two individuals tried to make their escape, one going to the side door and the other into the cab of the vehicle to exit by the passenger door.

By the time that we were able to grab one apiece we were all outside the vehicle and one almighty struggle commenced with a ready made audience of Eisteddfod goers. After rolling on the floor wrestling with one of them I saw that Phil had the other one pinned against the wall of the bridge and by this time I was dragging the other one to his feet. At this time we had no idea what if anything they had done, but it was obvious that they were up to no good. One thing was certain and that was that they were not women, they were now both totally disheveled and Phil's prisoner was without his wig.

As luck would have it a police motor cyclist was near to the scene and having seen the commotion came across to the van which enabled me and Phil to walk the two prisoners to the near by Police Station, leaving the motorcycle colleague to look after the van until it could be recovered for further inquiries to be made.

On entering the charge room, the duty sergeant asked why we had arrested them, to which Phil replied in his broad welsh accent, "For pretending to be bloody women!", to which the sergeant replied, "Since when has that been an arrestable offense?". To which Phil replied, "Today, but assault police will do."

Then came the searching of the prisoners which proved that they were definitely men, both wearing a complete set of women's clothing and bras stuffed with moulded bread cakes. There were documents on them with their male identities and they both turned out to be from the Torquay area. Further enquiries revealed that the van had been stolen from Torquay and was owned by a local person who had prepared and replenished his van for a day selling his hot dogs on the sea front, little did he think then that his bread cakes and sausage would be eaten in North Wales.

The van was eventually brought to the police station and searched and further property of the prisoners was found together with a considerable amount of money that they had taken. The cleanliness of the van itself left a lot to be desired after our two transvestites had obviously slept in it and, if the Eisteddfod goers who had purchased and eaten the goods had seen from where the food came they would have been making the same trip as the Chief Inspector did earlier.

After contacting the police at Torquay the owner of the van traveled up to collect it with two detectives to collect the prisoners to later appear at their hometown court.

The happenings of the day for Phil and I certainly lived up to performances of the day to be remembered.

DISPOSING OF THE BODY

It was a dark Autumnal night and I was on night duty, 10.00p.m. until 6.00a.m., the night Sergeant was Llew Roberts and, I was rostered to cover the surrounding areas to the divisional headquarters. I was to patrol with an officer I was in digs with by the name of Jim, but I had some reports to do and therefore I was allowed one hour to get them done and Jim would return for me in the van and then at the same time take Llew Roberts home for his usual sleep before setting off again to the surrounding towns and villages.

At 11.00p.m. Jim called at the police station and collected me and the Sergeant and our first port of call was the Sergeants house where as usual we dropped him off only to hear his usual rhetoric, "Pick me up at half past five.". He always reminded us as if we had never done it before and, then of course we had to arrange our night duty around him, anyway we set off on our way to patrol the surrounding areas.

As we reached certain points on our patrol we would make ourselves available at agreed times at certain telephone booths to receive calls should our presence be required anywhere, as there were no personal radios at that time and therefore that was the only form of contact available, it so happened that there was a radio in the vehicle that we were in, but contact with headquarters could not be made because of the mountainous area we were in.

It was now 1.30a.m. and we pulled up at a designated telephone booth. We had planned to eat our packing up there and should there be a call, answer it. As we stopped the telephone was already ringing non-stop, and I went to answer it and, as expected it was the headquarters switchboard and on having answered it I was told that a body had been spotted in the river at the next market town we were due to patrol and that the body was on our side of the river. The switchboard officer also told me that he had telephoned the Sergeant at home and that he was waiting to be picked up, but again not in the best of moods after being awakened from his sleep.

The river was the dividing line between counties and, the body being found on our side meant that it fell to us to deal with the sudden death and for one of us to be appointed the Coroner's Officer. It also meant that it would fall to us to get the body out of the water, examine it and remove it to the hospital or to the mortuary. We had already been told by the station that it was obvious that whoever it was dead.

We collected the Sergeant who was not in the best of moods. I got out of the passenger seat to make room for him and climbed in the back of the van for the ensuing seven or eight mile journey sitting most uncomfortably on the wooden lath seats.

On our arrival at the bridge the man who had spotted the body was still there, cold and wet as it had now started to rain. He showed us from the bridge where the body was, within some reeds and it was quite apparent that someone would have to paddle into the water to recover it. The river was quite fast flowing and it was dark and dreary and drizzling with rain.

The Sergeant directed his rhetoric to both me and Jim and said, "Get the man's name and address. He better get off home. He'll catch his death of cold.". Jim took his details and the Sergeant condescendingly thanked him and told him that someone would be round to see him at a later date.

As soon as the man was out of earshot and on his way home the Sergeant turned to me and said, "Go into the police station and get the rope from under the charge room counter.". We were covering the area because the police station was not manned every night of the week, and this was one of those nights. We had a key for the station which was very near to the bridge and with the aid of my torch found the key in the van, walked to the station door and opened it. It took a minute or two to find the light switch and sure enough the rope was found under the charge room counter, which I got and went out through the door, locked it and walked back to the scene.

The Sergeant and Jim were both standing on the bank of the river near to where the body was, there was no-one else about and the weather hadn't improved. The Sergeant turned to me and said, "It's only shallow there, wade in and pull him to here.". I said, "Wont there be any leggings or Wellingtons in the station?" to which he replied, "No, and in any case we haven't got time. Just pull it to the side!". I put my trousers inside my socks and waded in and, as soon as the water went above the lace level of my boots I could feel the water oozing in, it was cold and uncomfortable, but I carried on going until the water reached my knees. The bottom of the river was of rock and I was concerned that at anytime I could step out into space and end up at the bottom of the river. I turned and shouted to wards the bank, "Serg. Shouldn't I have the rope round me, it gets deep all of a sudden?" There was a shout back, "Just grab the body and pull it here. The ropes for him!". It didn't register what he meant, so I just reached out and grabbed the coat that was on the body, at first it didn't move, but after a few more tugs it came away from the reeds towards me.

With the body having been released it became difficult to steer it towards the bank because of the flow of the river and with having to turn around to face the bank, eventually I turned and still having hold of the coat managed to get the body to the bank. I was cold and exhausted with the body against the bank and my feet still in the water.

It was obvious that the person had been dead for some time and his saturated clothes was making the body hard to deal with and the flow of the river was making it even harder and, I had to keep a tight hold of the clothing. The Sergeant then said to me at the same time as handing me the rope, "Here you are, tie this round him.". I reached for the rope as I was hanging on to the body as best that I could and, at the same time noting that I was getting no physical help from the Sergeant or Jim. They were making no effort to put a foot into the water to assist.

I wrapped the rope under the arms with great difficulty and tied it as tight as I could and with the weight of the rope getting heavier, the wetter it got. I then said to the two of them on the bank, "That's as tight as I can get it, so you can pull it onto the bank now.". The Sergeant then shouted, "No. Just pull it towards the bridge and you (meaning me) paddle along with it to the bridge.", the bridge being about 10 yards away. They started pulling and I was paddling along, by this time I was holding a foot and ankle and noting the foot was without a shoe. We reached the bridge which was arched with a number of arches under the bridge against which you could hear the flow of the river being divided.

The Sergeant went up the bank onto the beginning of the bridge and at the same time he told Jim to follow him with the rope. He then turned towards where I was standing with my boots full of water and still holding onto the body, and said, "When we start pulling it across the river push the body out into the middle, we want to get it to the other side then it isn't ours to deal with.". Needless to say the penny had now dropped that the Sergeant's plan all along was to have the body found on the opposite bank so that officers of the neighbouring force would have to deal with the incident.

By this time the Sergeant and Jim were on the bridge with their end of the rope and the Sergeant shouted, "Push it out now as far as you can and we'll pull it across." I did as I was told and pushed the body out into the river and, I could see that they had taken the strain because the rope was being pulled tight, but that was partly because of the flow of the river which was running towards the bridge from the side that the body was on.

I pulled myself onto the bank with my feet squelching in the water that was in my boots and with my soaked trousers sticking to me. I could hear the voices of the Sergeant and Jim on the bridge and the Sergeant shouting, "Keep a tight grip on that rope!", and Jim replying, "It's a hell of a weight and it's against the pillar and I'm trying to pull it off." I could just see that the body was against the first pillar and there were another two to go.

I scrambled up the bank and squelched my way to where they were and, I could see that they were having extreme difficulty in holding onto the rope and pulling to the other side of the bridge at the same time. Jim then shouted, "We've reached the second pillar. It must be hard against it because it's got lighter.". I then looked over the side of the bridge and could just make out why the rope was lighter, because all that was on the end of the rope was an arm, the rest of the body had gone. The body had obviously been in the river long enough to dismember particularly with the strength of the flow and with it having collided with the pillars. I shouted to be heard over the noise of the river, "There's only what looks like an arm left on the rope.". Then the Sergeant looked over the side and shouted, "Bloody hell, pull it to the other side as quick as you can." He then went off to the other side himself and went down the bank to the edge of the river shouting to us, "Hurry up and get it over here.". By now I was helping Jim and we together managed to reach the other side and, still keeping the rope tight went down the bank to where the other end of the rope was and, to where the Sergeant was now standing.

The Sergeant turned to me and said, "Your feet are already wet so just get it onto the bank." Once again I had to paddle into the water and recover the dismembered limb and put it on the bank. The Sergeant then tried to undo the rope but couldn't because the knot was too tight with being wet. He then said, "We want a knife. Have you got one?". As luck would have it Jim produced one and handed it to the Sergeant, who then with some difficulty cut through the rope and handed the end to Jim saying, "We'll put that rope in the van and get rid of it later. The arm can stay this side in those reeds, So just put it amongst them and we'll get to the other side.". Needless to say it was me who was delegated to secure the arm amongst the reeds, which I did with the greatest of speed just to get out of the way.

The three of us made our way across the bridge with the Sergeant saying, "It's theirs now no matter where the rest of it is found. Put that rope in the van and we'll go into the station.". Jim threw the rope into the van and we walked the few yards to the station. I still had the keys, so I opened the door, went in and put the light on.

The Sergeant went straight to the telephone board and plugged in to the neighboring force, with whom there was a direct line from the station. The call was obviously answered and the Sergeant identified himself and said, "We've just been patrolling the area from our divisional headquarters and been stopped by a member of the public who has told us that there is part of a body on your side of the river. We trespassed into your county to have a look and, sure enough there does appear to be a limb or something in the reeds. We're now in our station and will wait for you to send someone so that we can show them where it is. How long will it take you to get someone here?". A few seconds later the Sergeant came off the telephone saying, "They wont be long, they've got someone nearby." He then turned to me and said, "You better get into the van while we stay in here until they come and we'll walk across the bridge with them. We can't have them seeing that you're soaked after being in the water." Dutifully I went to the van to await the arrival of the Sergeant and Jim after they had met the officers from the neighboring force. It was some three quarters of an hour before they came to the van and, in the meantime I was freezing sitting in the back of the van. I had tried to get my boots off, but they seemed to be glued to my socks and feet. I managed to get my trousers out of my socks and saw that my legs were black from the dye in them. I just resigned myself to sit there and wait.

On their return to the van the Sergeant said, some what triumphantly, "Well that's theirs now. We'll just call and see that fellow who found it and put his mind at rest and, tell him that the body just floated away to be found another day and then he wont be calling at the station to find out what happened."

It was gone 6.00a.m. by now and, with the knowledge that no-one had witnessed our actions we called at the informants home to find that he hadn't been to bed, but had copious cups of tea laced with a modicum of whisky. He invited us in and offered us a cup of tea, which I truly could have done with to put some warmth in me, but the Sergeant refused on behalf of all three of us. He then went on to again thank him in the most condescending way for his public spirited actions and told him that he didn't think that he would be required to be seen again, but if it was necessary then he would be called on. He was most grateful that we had called and, we left the house and climbed into the van to travel back to the division headquarters to go off duty.

On the way back I was stuck in the back of the van shivering and, being lectured together with Jim who was driving, by the Sergeant about the "Ways and Means Act", that being that if there is no written way of dealing with a matter then you use your initiative and least said the better with the appropriate record in your note book leaving out all the salient points. It was a first class lesson in how to be idle and deceitful by someone who had specialized in it for almost thirty years.

I was never more pleased to sign off duty at the station and walk the short distance back to the digs with Jim, both of us saying that that was a lesson NOT to be remembered.

It was some six weeks later that the body was found about three miles further down the river and the incident dealt with by officers from the neighbouring force and, at the inquest there was an Open Verdict given and reported in the local paper. It so happened that on the night of the report in the paper Jim and I were on night duty again with Sergeant Llew Roberts in charge and he took me and Jim to one said saying, "Have you both seen the report in the paper about the inquest on the fellow found in the river". We both said, "Yes!", and he went on to say, "Well you now see that's the way to do it. Go and get the van to take me home to pick me up at half past five and, don't call me out any earlier tonight!".

ONE STEP TOO MANY

Night shift was usually quiet, but the time of year always changed things particularly during the winter when the sea was crashing against the sea wall on the promenade, when the wind was strong and noisy as it was blowing through the trees and buildings and, blowing the rain against windows and walls. On occasions of such weather it always seemed colder and it was then that one appreciated the "Dog Collar" tunic, because you could wear a thick sweater underneath and then your overcoat and cape to keep warm.

It was such a night when I paraded for duty at 10.00p.m.to find that all the officers on parade were making the most of the warmest uniform clothing that they had. The weather was atrocious and I was detailed to patrol the beat which covered the centre of the town. Albeit that it was only a short distance from the station to the beat I found that I was soaked and having to fight against the wind with the noise of the wind and the noise of the sea being the only sound that could be heard. Any other noise would disappear into oblivion.

Over the previous few months there had been a number of shops broken into on the beat and the burglar remained at large. There seemed to be no pattern in the type of premises that were being targeted, so it was essential that all properties were checked thoroughly.

The weather made the night particularly dark and the wind and rain made the trip around the beat difficult. The street lights were poor and the use of the torch was necessary despite some of the shop premises having left the lights on.

There was virtually no-one about apart from the odd car traveling along the A56 which was the main coast road and went straight through the middle of the beat. The lighting was better along that road, but it was virtually pitch black in the side roads. I covered the beat as best as the weather would permit during the first half of the shift and then returned to the station at 1.00a.m. for my break, to have a warm drink and my packing up. I was drenched and was pleased to get my cape and overcoat off because of the weight caused by them being so wet. The others who were "Grubbing" at the same time were in the same predicament and it was a case of us all trying to get the best drying spot in the parade room where we satisfied our thirst and hunger.

The three quarters of an hour break soon passed, and it was on with the coats and the capes to brave the elements yet again. I walked to the beginning of my beat which was only some three or four minutes away, the weather had not improved and the noise of the elements was still deafening.

I got onto the beat only to be met by one of my fellow officers who had been covering his own beat and mine while I was taking refreshments, he was due to have his refreshments following me and I was to cover his beat, but the situation had changed. The fellow officer had crossed from his beat onto mine to work his way towards the police station and despite the noise and the visual impairment of the elements he came across an individual with a haversack who tried to discard it on seeing him and, at the same time started to run in the opposite direction. Despite the odds against a capture because of the protective clothing being worn by the officer he caught the individual and held him purely to check out his reactions after what was said to be a brief struggle.

The colleague had taken the detainee back to where he had seen him throw the haversack and recovered it, only to find that it was full of cigarettes and chocolates. The prisoner as he now was volunteered that he had broken into the Cigarette and Chocolate Cabin which was situated in the road leading to the station. I assisted the officer with the prisoner over the short distance back to the police station and, then returned to my beat with the task of patrolling my beat and that of the arresting officer.

The first need was to make the Cigarette and Chocolate Cabin secure which was done with the help of a couple of railway workers who were working nights and, were delighted to have a change of duty. They soon found a suitable piece of plywood and sufficient nails to cover the broken glass in the door of the Cabin until the premises were visited by the proprietor and the glass repaired. When the repair was being done the noise of the hammering of the nails was not heard over the noise of the sea, wind and rain, showing what an incredibly terrible night it was and, certainly not a night to face the weather scene. In retrospect it was a perfect night to commit such a crime and to make as much noise as was wanted and not be heard.

The time had past into the last two hours of duty and, what with dealing with the weather and the arrest of the burglar who one could surmise had been responsible for the burglaries which had been committed in the area in the recent past, I decided to have a five minute break on patrol by retiring into a doorway of a grocery shop which was set back off the pavement in the darkest street on the beat and have a "Quick drag." (In those days I did smoke the occasional one).

I was out of the rain and the wind was howling past the doorway, at least I was not being blown away for a few minutes and neither was I getting any wetter, as if I could!, but the noise of the weather was still deafening.

As I got settled in the doorway, I threw my cape back over my shoulder to search for the pocket which contained the cigarettes and matches and, I eventually found them in my tunic pocket. If per-chance I'd have been caught smoking on duty then that would have been regarded as a cardinal sin, but I was pretty confident that I wouldn't because everyone was engaged on patrol or seeing to the prisoner who undoubtedly was being interviewed about the shop breaking for which he had been caught and the others that had been committed over the previous months. Therefore I was going to relax for five minutes and contemplate the present and the future whilst having a fag.

I was just about to light up when I sensed a shuffle above me and at the same time a shoe caught me at the side of the head, clipping my ear and landing on my shoulder. What the hell was happening?. The burglar had surely been caught earlier, so what was this?. I looked up and there saw yet another shop breaker climbing backwards through the fan -light above the shop door trying to drag a bag of goods with him. Instinct took over and, shouting above the noise of the weather, "What the bloody hell's happening?", by this time his foot was off my shoulder and he was floundering to place his step onto the door handle to assist him in getting out. I was able to oblige in so helping him with a gentle tug at his leg which caused him to let go of his bag and, in doing so land in a heap between me and the door and, his "Goody bag" fell inside. On the landing there was a bit of a gasp of pain and the instinctive holding of the painful areas, that in this case being the back and knee.

The intruder had broken the fan-light when entering and the glass had fallen into the shop and he had climbed up the door, using the door handle as a foothold, then cleaned the glass out so as not to cut himself, thrown his bag in and then climbed in head first - pretty agile!.

Obviously the weather had fooled us both - the burglar not seeing me and me not seeing him in consequence of the darkness and noise caused by the weather- hence him, "Taking one step too many, that step being to rest on my shoulder."

I took hold of the individual having taken my handcuffs from the hanging position from the pocket of my overcoat and, for the first time of using them in my service I slapped them onto the wrists of the prostrate prisoner, he already had one hand behind his back so it was a matter of course for that wrist to be manacled first and the second wrist followed as a matter of course (I wish all such exercises were to be as simple in future such experiences).

I got the prisoner to his feet with continuing protest from him about his injured knee, which I couldn't feel and, quite honestly disregarded because my interest was to usher the felon to the station which was near by The premises were reasonably secure and I had no means of summonsing help so we set off to traverse the short distance to the station, I couldn't take his "Goody bag" with me because that was inside the locked door of the grocery shop to be recovered later.

On reaching the station with the prisoner still limping and moaning about his knee and also his back at this stage, I entered the charge room soaking wet, as was the prisoner and, quite exhausted because it felt that I had carried him up the hill from my beat to the police station. On having entered the police station it was obvious that the duty sergeant was tying up the loose ends following the arrest of the first villain and now completing the necessary paper work after lodging him in a cell. The sergeant looked up and exclaimed, "What the bloody hell have you brought him in for?".

I nearly felt guilty about the arrest, giving the sergeant more work, strangely it seemed to be something that they were not fond of. I then with some haste explained the circumstances of the arrest only to hear him shout, "That can't be right I've just sent the town center burglar to the cells, where the bloody hell has he come from?". All I could say was, "Out of the grocery shop window using my shoulder as a step to safety after having done it.". There was an immediate response, "What were you doing in the bloody doorway, having a fag?". To which I replied with some trepidation, "No. Trying the bloody door and what he's nicked is still in the shop just inside the door, because he dropped it as he was getting out after I helped him to the ground and that's why he has injured himself.". The response at least had a result in that there was then a silence which led up to the sergeant saying, "Stand there! (That being directly in front of him.). The prisoner shuffled up the charge room counter to be in front of the sergeant and then answered the personal detailed questions that were reigned upon him. After being booked in the prisoner was lodged in the cells and I went to get my wet clothes off before interviewing him further.

Before seeing the prisoner again I spoke to the other officer who had arrested the first shop breaker. He had collated all the information about the previous break-ins in the town centre and questioned his prisoner about them. There had been twenty five in all which included the one that his felon had committed prior to his arrest, he had listed every one of the break-ins and he gave me a copy of them (It wasn't a case of running the information off on a computer in those day) for which I was thankful. His prisoner had admitted thirteen of the offenses and would not hear of having committed any more. The ones that he had admitted were marked off on the sheet that had been given to me.

With a colleague I went to see my prisoner in his cell (there being no special interview rooms) and, having introduced myself and my colleague I inquired about his injuries and whether or not he wanted medical assistance, which he didn't. He was duly cautioned and he readily admitted the offense for which he had been arrested and, really he had no option so to do. With the shop breaking that he had been caught committing added to a total of twenty six shop break-ins in all, over the previous few months in the center of the town.

The prisoner told us that he had ventured on his criminal activities that night because of the weather with the knowledge that any noise caused by breaking in would be drowned by the noise of the weather and the sea. He then went on to explain what a fool he felt at not seeing me in the doorway and, even more so at trying to use my shoulder as a stepping stone. He then told us how he had seen me walking towards the police station earlier and that he presumed that I was going in for a break, so he thought the time was right and he went to the property which he had previously viewed with a view to breaking in. He entered via the fan-light, because it was above the eye level and not likely to be noticed straight away from outside the shop. He was dead right about that!. We asked him what he had in his bag, to which he replied, "Cigarettes.". We hadn't recovered the bag by this time because we were experiencing some difficulty in contacting the key-holder, who was either in an extremely deep sleep or choosing not to answer his telephone after having anticipated that he may have to go out and brave the elements. Eventually we did make contact and on him attending at the shop the bag was recovered full to the brim with cigarettes.

We then went on to question him about previous break-ins in the area and every one was put to him and, he admitted the twelve that the other prisoner had not. What a coincidence, thirteen a piece and, both caught on the thirteenth venture. Neither of the prisoners were known to each other and both were breaking in to steal the same sort of goods, namely cigarettes, chocolates and cash if it was about.

They were both charged with the offenses committed on the night in question and a number of the others and, the remainder were put to the Court to be taken into consideration when sentenced. All the break-ins were cleared up on a night that no-one would even dream of seeing anyone, never mind catching two prolific burglars. In essence both of them had "Taken one step too many.".

THE IRISH (S)MILE

It was a bright summers day, mid afternoon, plenty of holiday makers about and a heavy volume of traffic on the A56, the main coast road through the town of the divisional headquarters. On such a busy day it was the duty of the officer covering the beat in the center of the town to engage himself on traffic duty on the pedestrian crossing at the junction of the A56 and the road leading to the railway station, stopping traffic to let the pedestrians across and at the same time trying to maintain a steady floe of traffic. It was on this certain day that it fell to me to be the officer appointed to the town center beat. It was one particular duty that I detested, there was always the irate motorist to contend with and, it was little wonder that they were irate because of the holiday makers who were using the crossing and, being so dilatory in doing so.

On stopping the traffic to let the pedestrians over, there was always the odd one who wanted to ask directions which would automatically delay proceedings and, on having beckoned traffic on there was also the motorist who would stop and ask why he or she had been stuck in the traffic queue for so long and be a candidate for the "Road Rage Competition" in doing so.

The traffic queue on this particular day was phenomenally long and stretched back along the A56 to the adjoining town which was some three miles away and traveling at "Snails Pace". Nothing more could be done other than to usher the "Couldn't care less pedestrians" across as quickly as could be and spur the motorists on as best you could. Matters got worse, because of a visit from the duty sergeant to my point of duty to inform me that the next seaside town on the coast road, some five miles away, was also blocked with traffic and, that town being in the neighboring force area could not be controlled by us.

Frustration pitch was at a high, the pedestrian traffic was increasing and, because of the little movement of the vehicles they were treating the crossing of the road as if they had automatic right of way to the motorists. The motorists were wanting to creep forward to cover every yard that they were able and if a pedestrian was in the way, the horn would be blasted or there would be an angry shout. The heat of the day wasn't helping and, the angry shouts could be heard clearly because of the car windows being open of a necessity in the heat

I was wishing that I was in any place other than standing in the middle of a pedestrian crossing on the A56, in mid-summer with such a density of traffic and pedestrian holiday makers.

My back was to the traffic and I was letting the holiday makers over the crossing when there was "one hell of a bang", it was obviously a vehicle colliding with a vehicle in front of it and, on turning around to face the traffic I saw that a short wheel based lorry towing a caravan of some age had collided into the car in front. Everything, vehicular traffic wise, came to a sudden stop and, pedestrian wise all eyes were on the accident scene.

"Oh hell!". I straight away stopped all traffic coming towards me and left an open way across the road to the holiday makers and, I then walked the few paces to the collision. The driver of the car that had been hit was standing there, he was furious, shouting, "What the F---ing hell have you done?". In the broadest of southern Irish accents, if you could understand it, came, "It is with me being terribly sorry that the traffic is going so slow that my clutch has failed and the lorry did jump forward without me doing anything and, it has to be sure made a terrible mess at the back of your wheels".

The car driver was extremely emotional, meandering about in the immediate vicinity, taking his head in his hands and, asking the question, "Should that Irish idiot be behind a wheel, behind the wheel of any vehicle, never mind such a tip of a lorry like that?"

One only had to look at the vehicle to know straight away that the vehicle was not fit to be on the road. In the cab after the driver had alighted was a female, possibly his wife?, and a lad of about fifteen years of age and, there was the inevitable dog. The stench was just something not to be experienced, stale tobacco from rolled "Fags", body sweat and with the heat of the day making it even worse. On the back of the truck was everything, a bit of tarmac, old doors, copper, lead, an old fireplace and miscellaneous junk.

I asked the driver of the car to remain with his vehicle until I'd had a word with the Irish itinerant and dealt with the traffic as best I could until some assistance arrived. On then looking towards the dilapidated caravan being towed, two of the windows were opened and little heads were poking out and the door had also been opened by another small child, all three of them were making their presence felt by their vocals.

I went to the driver of the lorry and said, "I'm going to have to get you pulled into one of the side roads if I can find space, so that we can sort this out. Is that your Mrs in the lorry?". "Aye, it is." he replied, and being concerned about the children, I said, "Will you go and ask her to get them together with her and take them into the church gardens to sit there in the shade of the trees?" (the Parish Church was just at the side of the accident and the gardens were always beautifully kept). "Aye, I will that." he said, and continued, "The rest of the kids can sit there with them with their mams', they're in the wagons behind us.".

On looking back I could see a good number of similar vehicles in the traffic queue interspersed with the holiday traffic. I said, "How many of them are there?", to which he replied, "About seventeen. We're on our way to the ferry to make the crossing across the water to our granddad's wake and we stick together in case we need any help on the way. We'll be back in about a month.". Why he should have told me that I just didn't know and, the last person I wanted to see in a months time was him.

The next questions were purely routine, "What's your name?". "Mick Smith.", was the reply. What's your address?". "Well we live in the wagon and the van at the back and it could be anywhere we stop.".

"Can I see your driving license and insurance please?". The reply must have been practiced over a number of years, "I lost me license and I've sent off for another one.". "Where have you asked them to send it to?". "Well we were staying in Durham at the time in a field that had a post box and they must have sent it there, we'd have been back there by now but for me granddad dieing so I'll have to wait till I go back to be getting it.". "Can I see your insurance certificate please?". "Aye, well that's the same, me and the rest of the family in all those wagons are insured together and we're waiting for the papers to come through. It's hard yer know because non of us can read nor write."

By this time I was in a state of desperation, with the traffic at a total stand still, and an irate driver who had heard my conversation with "Mick Smith" and, who realizedthat there wasn't going to be any recompense for the damage caused to his vehicle. At the same time as asking the routine questions, I took a cursory glance at the Road Fund License only to find that displayed within the holder was a Guiness bottle label being disguised as the Road Fund License "What's this?", I asked pointing to the purported Road Fund License. "Ah well, with going back to Ireland we didn't want to be spending the money on them, so we put them there because we didn't want there to be anyone thinking that we were getting away without paying for the traveling on the roads to the ferry.".

This was an impossible task!, but assistance arrived from the near by police station in the shape of Sergeant Llew Roberts and two constables, needless to say Llew Roberts took the stance on the soap box, doing nothing himself, but directing, by then, us three officers on how to clear the traffic at the same time as dealing with the accident involving the gypsies.

The strategy was to hold up the traffic traveling from the west to enable the holiday traffic traveling in the opposite direction to make up some ground after having been stationary for so long and, bring all the Irish lorries with their caravans together on the main road, for them to be together and dealt with and, to enable the holiday and local traffic to be guided past as best they could be with stop/go signals at convenient points

We started on the west bound traffic and managed to assist on their way all the traffic squashed between the tinker's vehicles and, bring together the Irish convoy of vehicles of various description, be it lorries and vans of untold sizes , shapes and condition. The caravans and trailers they were towing were even worse, descriptions beggared belief. It was an immediate scene of a vehicle scrap yard being deposited on the A56 within minutes, it was difficult to believe that the vehicles were able to move, but they did!. There was no side road for them to go, there was nothing left to do but to continue to move the traffic past the convoy by stopping one direction and allowing them through and then the other, and the tinkers remaining together on the main coast road until all accident details had been completed. There was also the enraged car driver to pacify, who obviously knew what his position was by now, he was still fuming, but that didn't assist in anyway, but thank goodness he was sensible enough to know that the best course of action was for us to contact him at a later date with the details of the offending driver (if there were any). His details had been taken and he was guided to the nearest garage for the repairs that were immediately necessary, so thankfully that immediate problem was over.

Having dealt with the car driver I could see that Mick's wife, if she was, was with kids in the church yard, in the shade and, she was being joined by all the other wives and kids from the other lorries and vans, it was total bloody chaos with the children running all over and shouting at being together and free and a decibel count would have confirmed that ear drums were in danger of being damaged. At least they were safe!.

Now the problems started, we eventually managed to return all drivers' to their respective vehicles, that was me and Llew Roberts, because the other two officers were directing the traffic and holiday makers which didn't seem to let up, but at least there was movement in each direction.

The Sergeant, in a style that only he had, then said to me, "Well, the traffic's moving and the kids are safe. You check all the drivers and the vehicles while I keep a watch on how the traffic is moving and, get the bloody lot of them on the move as quick as you can into the next force area because they've got to see them to the boat. I'll go up to the station and ring them to tell them what's on the way (once again it was the "Ways and Means Act" written by Sergeant Llew Roberts.

Mick Smith was wrong, there weren't seventeen followers, but twenty two in total, as others piled up behind those that were already convoyed with the hope that they could be got away as soon as possible. They all had to be seen and, would you believe, every one of them had the surname of "SMITH", the forenames were those that they thought appropriate to the occasion, non of them had a driving license that they could produce and, they were all subject to the block insurance for which they were expecting papers at an unknown address in Durham, or so they said. They were all issued with tickets to produce their documents at a police station within fourteen days. What a fruitless exercise!. They were all going to disappear to their homeland without any thought of producing any documents or of being responsible for the disruption caused. It was amazing to find that every one of the vehicles had Guiness bottle labels displayed and disguised as Road Fund Licenses, but they all with the greatest of assurance of speech positively stated that it was their intention to produce their documents within the required period of time, as one can guess that assurance was not believed.

All the vehicles should have been taken off the road there and then, but what do you do, there was no where to impound the vehicles and vans, there was no-where to accommodate the kids and, there was no facility to investigate further the families. The Smith family being one hell of a size. What a mess!.

It was a thankful appearance of Sergeant Llew Roberts that solved the matter, he having made the appearance in style in the divisional road traffic patrol car, being driven by the traffic patrol officer down the centre of the two lane carriageway to the front of the Irish convoy. He alighted from the car and immediately took charge by saying to me, "Have you got all their details lad?", to which I replied, "Yes, but all the vehicles want examining and non of them have any driving licenses or insurance with them.". It was Llew's presence in the heat of the day, portly standing there, in his dog collared uniform which was smartly creased and displaying his numerous medal ribbons, together with the waving of his pacing stick that commanded everyone's attention when he replied to me, "Well let's get these good Irish folk on their way. All the ladies and children back into their vehicles and vans and on their way. P.C. Jones (the driver of the patrol car) will escort them to the boundary for the next force to take them to the ferry."

The boundary was only some four or five miles away and once again Llew Roberts had passed the buck, for me to know of, for ultimately the Irish police to deal with if they so cared and, it was with that that he turned to me and said, "Well, that will give them something to do, anyway it's out of our patch."

Reality had arrived, stuff them all back into the vehicles together with the dogs that had peed up every lamp-post and deposited their droppings where-ever and send them on their way.

They were indeed escorted to the force boundary and nothing was heard of them thereafter, but they made their mark as being those responsible for the biggest traffic jam in North Wales, it being in excess of many miles and, the outcome being with Irish smiles, they never being seen again, but the poor driver involved in the collision having to confront his own bill for the damage caused, and not a single prosecution in sight.

What a day caused by the Irish (S)mile(s)!".

After that experience it was no wonder that I wanted my career to progress in any other direction than being engaged with traffic incidents and scenes, particularly if the Irish were to be involved.

THE FENCE AND BALL-RACE
EXPERIENCE

Whenever there was an emergency call for an ambulance to a scene of an incident which resulted in a person being taken to hospital as a result of the incident then the police were always informed in-case there was any criminal offense involved.

I was on a late duty, 2.00p.m. to 10.00p.m., designated to patrol the towns and areas around the divisional headquarters with a colleague, Jeff, in the divisional Bedford van which was still in its dilapidated state and somehow still managing to survive the axe, when we made an arranged `point` call to the station to see if we were required anywhere in particular. We were wanted, the officer on telephone duty telling us, "A man has been taken to the hospital from work and, the circumstances of his arrival in the casualty department and his condition is said to be somewhat strange.". We were then on our way to investigate.

The time was about 9.00p.m., and the month was October, it was dark. The Bedford van had just had a siren fitted, which worked, but there was no blue light only a dimly lit `Police` sign above the windscreen. We raced to the hospital with the siren fully on, enjoying the experience of being able to experience vehicles giving way for us to pass and travel to our destination, but not having a blue light to show where the noise of the siren was coming from didn't assist, particularly because it was dark.

When my colleague and I arrived at the hospital we realized why the officer on telephone duty had received such a guarded message from the hospital which was eventually passed to us. It would have been inappropriate for the message to have been, "There's a fella at the hospital with his cock stuck in a ball-race.". The message in those terms possibly wouldn't have been believed anyway.

Sure enough, on our arrival at the hospital we found that there was a person in one of the cubicles commanding more attention than anyone else. He was certainly being attended to and, he was positively the center of attraction to a wide audience of nurses and anyone else who could borrow a nurses' uniform to peep through the curtains of the cubicle to experience the sight of what was going on behind them. When we saw the obvious commotion we inquired of a male nurse, who had just alighted from the cubicle with tears of laughter rolling down his face, of what had been going on behind the drapes.

We were beginning to think that this poor nurse, who we knew from past experience was a first class nurse, had been subjected to tear gas or laughing gas, because he couldn't get his words out for laughing. Suddenly, amongst the laughter which the nurse was trying to disguise, he spluttered out to us, "He's got his cock stuck in a ball-race joint and, we can't move it.".

We couldn't believe our ears, our pace quickened towards the cubicle and we also went to view the scene. Yes, there was a room full of medics, with a poor young doctor in charge, a , who obviously had never experienced or encountered such a problem before. There lying on the cubicle bed was a man aged about thirty three with his penis protruding through what could only be described as a large stainless steel washer (previously referred to as a ball-race). The outer end of the ball-race was preventing the return of the penis because the penis had swollen and wouldn't allow its return, causing the swelling and discoloration of it to the deep shades of red and pale blue. He was obviously in great pain, because he was moaning and writhing about, totally oblivious to the attention and sight seeing that his condition was attracting.

Our concern was obviously for the well being of the patient and, we were asking the question of how he had been caused to arrive in such a situation?.

Was there someone else involved?. Had someone placed his penis in that position, knowing the consequences, to cause him injury because of some problem within a relationship or household?.

It was then found that he had been accompanied to the hospital in the ambulance by two work mates, who were in a state of disbelief, as were the hospital staff.

It occurred to me that there was no offense and never would be of indecently assaulting or raping a stainless steel ball race.

We got the two workmates into an interview cubicle and enquired of them as to what had happened, both of them appeared to be still in a state of shock and, one of them had his hands on his head repeating the words, "Queer bastard!"

The calmer of the two was then asked the straight question, "What has happened for you to have to bring him to hospital in that state?". "Well he'd been missing from his work bench for some time and we were all concerned so we decided to search the factory and, we found him in the toilet". Apparently he had only been found then because of the moans and groans that were coming from the other side of one of the cubicle doors in the gents' toilets. The door was locked and had to be forced open to gain entry only to find the missing worker and, now the patient, lying in a prostrate position on the floor supporting his penis with both hands and holding it aloft within a ball-race. The agony was such that the moans and groans were now at shouting pitch and, despite the efforts of the workmates, there was no-way that they were going to be able to release him from his agony. The blood pressure would not subside and the metal certainly would not give way.

Like the young doctor, the workmen had never previously experienced anything like it before, but when they found him they quickly guessed at the reason for his dilemma, because on the floor near to him was a magazine(needless to say he was not then reading it),it was however open on the center pages showing a full colour picture of a nude female.

The pain and suffering was obviously self inflicted and, we had nothing further to investigate other than to satisfy ourselves that he had not previously been involved in any indecent or perverted behaviour. That of course could not be ascertained until he had been released from the predicament that he was in.

The farce became even funnier to those who were present with him and to those who new what had happened, which by that time was virtually the whole hospital, when the fire-brigade turned up with cutting equipment together with three more work colleagues from the factory where he worked also armed with specialize cutting equipment. The imaginations were running wild and, the quips were numerous and the amusement of all could be seen at a glance at those present.

The patient was moved into an accident and emergency theatre, there to be treated by the doctor and his staff and two firemen who by now were suitably clad in an attire which suited the scene, needless to say they had their cutting equipment with them.

The operation took easily an hour, but he was eventually cut free and, the release was signified by the two firemen coming out of the theatre with one of them holding aloft fragments of the ball-race joint and shouting, "We've done it!", followed by a loud cheer. The medical staff did not show themselves as they were obviously putting the final touches to the successful surgery.

It by now was long gone our finishing time, albeit that we had let the station know the reason for our lateness, but they wanted the van for the night shift We were obviously not going to be able to have a few words with the patient, because he was recovering from the surgery, so we enquired of the male nurse as to whether or not the patient was being kept in over night. He said that he would be and, that they had informed his next of kin, his wife, to that effect. God knows what he was going to tell her. The male nurse then said, "I've checked the medical records and, he's (referring to the patient) been in before in May this year and, strangely it was an injury to his cock which he said he'd trapped in his zip. It makes you think doesn't it?"

I then said,"We're not able to see him tonight, but what time will he be discharged tomorrow?" The nurse replied' "Well he's not forced to be discharged tomorrow, but if he is it will be after the doctor's rounds which wont be until after four o'clock.". To which I replied, "Well we'll be back on duty again at two tomorrow, so can you mark your notes to that effect and, if he's going sooner will you let the station know.". That was agreed.

The following day both me and Jeff paraded for duty at 2.0p.m. and were designated the same patrol as the day before to facilitate us being able to see the hospital patient. Following the usual formal duty parade we went straight to the van to travel to the hospital and, on journeying there we were betting on the cause of the previous visit to the hospital, by the patient, we came up with all sorts of possibilities.

On entering the hospital we inquired as to which ward the patient was on and, the same male nurse was on duty and couldn't have been more helpful. He was also extremely inquisitive as to the real reason and circumstances of the patient's injury in May. After telling the ward that he was on he went on to say,"His wife came in after you had gone last night and, after she found out what had happened there was hell on. It was a good job he was sedated because she hurled a stream of abuse at him and then threw the medical board at him from the end of the bed, which just missed the site of the injury. He won't be going home today in any case, but I don't think he would be welcome in any event. Apparently his wife had left in a hurry informing him that his belongings would be waiting for him at home when he was discharged.

We went to the ward to find that the patient was out of bed sitting in a chair. We had a word with the ward Sister who was expecting us and, she told us that we could use one of the consultancy rooms to see the patient. We thanked her and, she went to summon her patient, who walked into the consultancy room with difficulty and displaying obvious discomfort. We introduced ourselves and, enquired of his well being, he said, "I've never been in so much pain as I was in last night. They gave me loads of pain killers after. It was all my fault, I was just trying to get a bit of a thrill."

That really completed the interview of the cause of the previous days incident and, that being out of the way, I said, "You seem to be finding yourself having quite a bit of bother with injuries to your penis, you were treated here last May in the Accident and Emergency Department for bruising, bleeding and soreness caused to the same area. You said you'd caught it in the zip of your trousers, what really happened?". He was obviously surprised that we knew of that visit in May that he had made to the Infirmary and he said, "How do you know about that?. It was as you said I caught it in the zip and I couldn't free myself."

It so happened that we had for some time been subjected in the area "to a Phantom Flasher", whose method of operating was to walk along the street, no matter how busy it was and just open his raincoat and expose an erect penis to females of no matter what age. There was no telling of what day or what time of day the offences would occur.

Jeff asked me to go with him to just outside the consultancy room door so that he could have a word with me, which I did. When outside the door Jeff said, "You know the spateof indecent exposures we've had in the area, well it was about May when I had a report from an irate middle aged lady that a man had indecently exposed himself to her. She'd been walking on the main road alongside the wooden fence which borders the tennis club when she heard someone from the other side shout, `Get hold of this`. She then looked in the direction from where the voice was coming and she saw an erect penis penetrating through a knot hole in the fence. She couldn't see anyone because the fence is about six and a half foot high. She had her umbrella with her and she swung at the offending penis only to hear someone scream. Nothing else was seen or heard, but the penis disappeared. I went with her for her to show me where it had happened and sure enough there was blood around the hole, so she had obviously injured him. The one thing I didn't do was check at the hospital, because I thought that it would be the last place that the `Flasher` would want to attend.". I said, "Bloody hell, I bet it's him!"

We went back into the room and sat down, the patient was obviously unsettled and, obviously uncomfortable and, we asked him if he was alright to answer a few more questions and, he said that he was.

Jeff then said, "You know when you hurt yourself in May I was on duty and a lady reported to me that someone had indecently exposed himself to her on the main road near to the tennis club and, we've had a number of such complaints. I think that that flasher could be you." The patient replied, "I just can't think what you're talking about. If ever I've done any thing , I've always done it on my own. I've never flashed!". I asked, "What do you mean by doing anything, do you mean that you've done other things?" "No, I've never done anything." he replied. "Well tell us again how you came by the injury to your cock in May of this year?". I've already told you!", he said, "I caught the f---ing thing in the zip.". "Oh, come on!", said Jeff, "I've caught mine in me trouser's zip, but it didn't end up with me being in hospital. It was painful, but on that occasion I was pissed and didn't end up in hospital.", said Jeff." You didn't end up in hospital because you were pissed, but you must have been in pain and know what it's like.", said the Interviewee. "Yes.", said Jeff, "But the fact is I didn't rush to hospital for treatment for my innocent injury, but if it was you that rushed to hospital after having your cock belted by an umbrella then we can check the blood sample taken from the scene with the blood sample taken when you came to the hospital and, your blood doesn't alter and we've got plenty of samples to work from now you have come into hospital again (there was no blood sample taken from the tennis club fence and neither was there DNA testing at that time, but he didn't know!).".

We waited for the reply, which came after an extremely worried pause and, one could see the extreme anxiety on his facial expression, but true to expectation he said, "What are you trying to do to me, me wife's told me I've had it. Me life's over. What's going to happen to the kids?. I've done f--- all and, I've told you about getting f---ed up in the bog, I don't want anything else. You know about that, but I don't want anything else."

Jeff then stood up saying, "I'll just have to go for the results.". I said, "What, the blood test results, will they be through so quick?", to which he replied, "Yes, because of the recent hospital samples that have been taken and they've promised me that they'll be here this afternoon, I'll see if there's been a telephone call..".

Jeff left the interview and, I continued to talk to the interviewee, (bearing in mind that there was no tape recording at that time) and, I was asking him about his family and work and trying generally to ease him, but it was difficult because he couldn't be still, despite his obvious pain from his tender parts. He was obviously expecting the results of the blood test to be sprung on him on Jeff's return. I obviously was aware that there weren't any blood testing results, but on Jeff's return into the room he declared, "Well the results show that there's a match between the blood on the tennis court fence and yours, so, it's beyond doubt that it was you who got your cock belted by an umbrella in May this year. What have you got to say now?".

As could be expected there was a positive silence and pause and, then a positive admission, "O'k, It was me. I just did it. I don't know why. I saw her coming down the road and had an urge on and did it. I didn't want to go to hospital, but it was bad after she hit me and, I've been worried ever since that they'd catch me because I went to the hospital.". Jeff just said, "Well we have!".

"Now then.", said Jeff, "Let's talk about all the other flashing you've done, we've had stacks of complaints and, on checking, (there hadn't been any checking up to then, but he didn't know and, there wasn't any proof that he'd been responsible), the description of the flasher is identical to you. It has been you hasn't it?". "Look if I say anything will me wife know, because if she does, that's the end.". "She knows already what happened yesterday.", said Jeff, "We're told that you got your orders to quit the home last night, so the relationship seems to be over, where have you got to go?". "I'll go to me mam and dads.", he said".

"Look, before you go anywhere, we want to know what you've been up to for some time, let's be getting to the bottom of it and that can only be done by you telling us and clean your slate. What has been happening?".

It was now the tears time , the weeping and the exclamations, "I don't know why I did it? I don't know what's got into me!".

We were totally unprepared for the admissions and, we had to then get back to the station to check the registers to know how many reports of indecent exposure there had been, when they'd been committed and where, so I said to him, "Apparently they're keeping you in tonight and, we've got to go down to the station to check a few things. If we get our checks completed soon enough we'll be back to see you later, but if they send you home we'll see you again at your home or at your mum and dads."

We then handed him back to the duty Sister by walking him back past her office, he was obviously walking with great difficulty, so we left him with the Sister directing him to his bed and he struggled off towards it with the Sister saying to us, "He wont be going anywhere for at least a week because he's soar, raw and in a pretty bad state at the moment around his privates, so if you want to see him again, feel free to call. He won't be running away, because he couldn't."

We went back to the station wondering how many reported crimes we had cleared up and, as soon as we got there we immediately went to the crime register and started our check, only to find that there had been twenty three in the previous eighteen months and, there was one which had progressed to an indecent assault. The indecent assault had happened following the `flashing`, because the young girl had been too petrified to move and the assailant had gone to her and grabbed her breasts.

As we were searching the crime register the Detective Inspector came into the room and enquired as to what we were doing, we told him and, on having told him of how many reported crimes we now suspected him of being responsible for, he said, "Get yourselves back up there and put them to him, we could do with a good clean up for our crime figures this month."

Armed with the crime reports we set off again for the hospital and, once again received the same accommodation from the duty Sister to interview. She was very worldly wise saying, "I knew you'd be back sooner rather than later. I've been watching him and, he's a very worried man and, so he should be, he nearly lost his tackle and may still do so.". She then beckoned her patient over from his chair and into the consultancy room, to where we were with our files.

It was difficult not to feel sorry for him as he came into the room, because he was obviously in some considerable pain and showed it by the grimace on his face. As soon as he entered the room he said, "I'm due some pain killers soon, so it should be better."

I said, "Well, our findings are not going to improve matters, particularly if our thoughts are proved to be correct. We're going to put certain happenings to you which we think you are responsible for and, then you can tell us if our thoughts are right or not. You know that you are under caution now and needn't say anything unless you wish to do so." Jeff then started to go through the crime reports of all the indecent exposures reported.

One by one they were ticked off as, "Yes, that was me.". All were included in his statement. Jeff then came to the `flashing accompanied with the indecent assault`, and having put that to him he said, "Yes it was me, she didn't move and seemed if she wanted me to do something." I said, "Didn't you ever think that she was so petrified that she couldn't move or say anything because of you?", to which the pathetic reply came, "No.".

We had now `got an answer to, or detected` twenty three indecent exposures and one indecent assault, which would certainly improve the crime detection rate and please those that had started to quantify efficiency by statistics.

Now having spent about three hours with the patient/interviewee we were naturally pleased with the outcome and, it having been decided that Jeff would be the charging officer and, Jeff telling him what he would be reported for, he said, "What about the others?".

We looked at each other and, I said, "What others?". The reply came, "Well I don't want you to come back and ask me about any more. I just want it all to be over. There are some more. They're all written down in a diary at home that I've kept in the shed so that she wouldn't see them. I can get it for you when I get out of here."

Jeff and me were taken aback and, I said to him, " We'll ask Sister if we can take you home to get the diary and, then we can bring you back here if that's alright with you?". To which he replied, "Yes, it's

O.K. by me." We asked the Sister for permission to take him home to recover the diary and, she agreed.

With the aid of a push chair we got him to the van and placed him in the most comfortable seat there was, which meant that I had to sit in the back, but he wasn't very comfortable, albeit that he had easy access to his injured parts via the dressing gown and pyjama trousers. We travelled to his home and, Jeff parked the van outside while I went to the door, I knocked and, the door was answered by the wife. I told her that her husband was in the van and we had just brought him to recover something from the shed and that we were then going to return him to the hospital, because his condition was not good. She then went off in a fit of verbal abuse, "Take that f---ing bastard from here. All his gear is in the boxes outside the shed and he can take the f---ing lot. I've cleared the house and the shed of his things. He's never coming back here.". She then handed to me a diary saying, "I found this in the shed, this is what he wants to give to you, if he doesn't then I'm giving it to you anyway. Don't let him out of that van or I'll kill him.". I then explained to her that arrangements would be made to collect his things and that someone would be round to tell her of the arrangements.

I couldn't get away fast enough. I retreated to the van and showed the prisoner (as he then was) the diary and, he confirmed that that was the book that he wanted to retrieve and hand to us, but all he could do was exclaim, "If she's read that then it's over, it's all over. I'll never be back!". Acting as a Job's comforter I said, "No, I don't think you will and, not being a betting man, I'd bet that you wont be returning there.".

The scene was departed as quickly as possible to return to the hospital and, to place our interviewee back in the safe caring hands of the ward Sister, but not before going through his diary with him. He had recorded in his diary every `flashing` that he had done and also put into writing his thoughts and feelings after having committed the offences. There was a self admission in his own hand writing in his own diary of all that he admitted to us and, there were another thirteen that had not been reported by the victims for some reason or another. It proved impossible to trace those victims who had not reported the crimes.

Needless to say, there was mounds of work to be done, to inform all the injured victims of the successful conclusion of the investigation, which eased them considerably and, eventually the culprit was discharged from hospital and, so I'm told extensively scarred. He duly appeared in court on five charges of indecent exposure (the rest were taken into consideration on the sentencing) and one of indecent assault and, albeit that it was his first appearance before a court he was sentences to six months imprisonment. What he's been up to since his release, is up to now beggars belief.

The fact remains that incidents he was guilty of caused innocent people a good deal of grief and, hopefully the fence and ball-race incidents scarred his thoughts and desires for any repeat of his behaviour in the future.

THE CHEESE WIRE
AMPUTATION

It was yet another night patrol and, within months of the "Fence and Ball-race Incident", when we were again summonsed to the same hospital, following a call that the divisional headquarters had received from the hospital that a man had walked into the casualty department, covered in blood showing to the front of his trousers and carrying the top one and a half inches of his penis in his hand.

I, again was on duty with Nigel and, covering the hospital area in the divisional Bedford van, which was in its usual dilapidated state and, we got to the casualty department as soon as we could.

On arrival, we could see that there a good deal of activity in one of the cubicles and, we could also see that the A & E Theatre was being prepared. Sure enough, behind the cubicle curtain was a man in his late twenties, being seen to by a couple of doctors together with their nursing staff. They were trying to stem the bleeding from the patient's penis (there was no micro-surgery in those days, so there was going to be little good come out of the preservation of the top one and a half inches), they were best left alone with the patient to enable them to get him into the theatre to do whatever they had to. Strangely, the patient didn't seem to be in much pain apart from telling the staff that it was stinging like hell.

We left the cubicle and went through the waiting room into the entrance where the Porter was, he was a chap we knew from calling at the place so often and, as we walked up to him he said, "That's about as strange as you can get, a bloke bleeding to death and carrying half his cock in his hand."

Our immediate thought was that some irate husband or lover had found him in a compromising position and wanted to make sure that he was not capable of doing anything in the future. If that was the case then we had a serious assault to deal with. We had managed to get his name and address from one of the nurses who had admitted him and, we were about to leave the hospital to visit relatives, when I said to the Porter, "You didn't see who brought him here did you?". To which he replied, "Yes, he came on his own, I was having a cig outside when he drove up. His van's just on the side there, I'm going to have to get it moved.".

We went out of the hospital entrance and, there was the van, would you believe `a bull nosed Bedford`, the same model as we were in, in a total state of degradation from the outside and obviously ready for the scrap heap, as was ours. The doors were unlocked, if the truth was known the locks most probably would not work, with Nigel at one door and me at the driver's side, we opened the doors virtually simultaneously. We then saw that there was blood splattered all over the inside of the vehicle. It was obvious that we had to have the vehicle taken to the police station to be further examined.

We used the services, at that time, of a local break down vehicle owner who was pretty efficient and, we went back into the hospital again to see the Porter to ask if we could use the telephone. He immediately obliged us, and Nigel said to him, "You wont have to move his vehicle because we are getting a break down vehicle to pick it up and take it to the station compound. They'll be here shortly to take it away, so if you wouldn't mind just keeping a watch on it until they come, they know what they're doing and when they pick it up they'll leave it at our compound for us.

Normally we wouldn't have left it, but we deemed it more urgent to enquire of the family as to what had been or could have been the cause of the injury. We went to the patient's home address, which proved to be the marital home, his wife was at work cleaning and, the kids who were aged about six and seven years were playing and being looked after by their paternal grandmother.

Grandma was surprised to see us and, on having ascertained that she was the patient's mother, we explained to her in the gentlest way possible what had happened. She was in a complete state of shock and couldn't help in anyway in telling us what the relationship was like between her son and her daughter in law. She said that all she did was baby-sit while they were at work and, that she didn't meddle in there relationship. She did say however that they'd been married for some eight years and that they had the two children and that they seemed to be relatively happy. We inquired as to when the wife would be home and, we were then told that she was expected at any time as of now.

It was within a matter of minutes that the wife of the patient arrived home and, she was more shocked than her mother in law was at seeing us. She immediately said, "What have the kids been up to?". We assured her that the children had not done anything and we were not present to inquire into them.

I then said to her, "It's about your husband who is in hospital, but his condition isn't life threatening, I wonder if me and my colleague can have a word with you on your own while gradma looks after the kids.". She said, "Yes, we can go in there (pointing to the front room). He's alright isn't he, he's not going to die, is he?". "No, he's not going to die, but we have to tell you what has happened to him and, then you can tell us if you can help to find out exactly what has happened.", I said.

We were all standing in the front room of the house and, I said, "Let's sit down and we'll tell you first what has happened to him, but I must say that it isn't very pleasant and, it could affect your relationship in the future, particularly your sexual relationship.". "What do you mean? He's always been good to me and the kids. We've known each other since we were fifteen. What's happened?".

Nigel was keeping particularly quiet, so it was left to me to explain the perplexing situation that had occurred concerning her husband and that to date there was no explanation for her husband's condition. "Look.", I said, "Your husband has obviously been out at work today in his van, is that right?". "Yes", she said, "He works as a postman and does odd jobs for people when he comes home after work and he uses his van when he's doing the jobs. It's extra money for us. What's happened to him? I need to know.".

"Just before we explain what has happened", I said, "Tell me if there has been any difficulty within your relationship?. Has there been any suspicion by you or your husband that there has been an affair going on, by him or by you?". "Don't be stupid, we've never had any problem and, we've been married for years and got two kids.", she replied with some venom.

Now came the telling time, "Look", I said, "We are here to help and investigate and, if your husband's injuries have been caused by someone then it amounts to a serious assault and, we need to find out exactly what has happened.". I decided that it was the time to keep talking and said, "I have to be absolutely blunt about your husband's condition, he went to the hospital this afternoon in his van, covered in blood holding part of his penis in his hand. He's now being prepared for surgery to correct the amputation, but by now he's most probably being operated on. We don't know how or why, where or when the amputation took place. We are wanting to find out Has there been any domestic difficulty?".

By this time she was totally in a state of shock saying, "Has he had his tail cut off?". "Yes, that's what it amounts to and, our question is, is someone responsible for it?. Have you or him been having an affair?. Has someone done it in a state of revenge? We haven't been able to talk to your husband, because he was being taken into the theater to be attended to.", I questioned. She was now in a total state of shock saying, "Tell me your joking!. Neither of us have ever been unfaithful. We've always been together. When can I see him?". Nigel then said, "We'll take you straight away, but we had to put those questions to you and tell you what we know up until now, because we haven't been able to speak to your husband and, we don't think that you will be able to talk to him much because he will be heavily sedated when we get to the hospital.". "I just want to see him, can we go now?". Yes was the answer and we set off with her to the hospital leaving grandma with an extended baby-sitting afternoon.

On reaching the infirmary we found that the van had been collected and, that the patient had had surgery and was now in the recovery ward prior to being taken to a staying ward to be cared for. We also ascertained, after inquiry, that there had been no reattachment of the amputated end and, furthermore that the patient was not going to be discharged for quite a few day. There was no chance that we were going to be able to talk to him that evening and, that we would make arrangements to see him the following day when we were both on duty again. We made the reception ward staff aware of our intentions to return the following day and, again spoke to the patient's wife, who was being comforted by the ward staff. She stated her intention of remaining at the ward until he was brought from the operation recovery area to see him and talk to him. She was still in a state of shock and disbelief, albeit that she had no idea of the cause of the injury and, come to that no-one else did, apart from the patient. She was in good hands so we left her there, not knowing what would be revealed.

The following day Nigel and I were again on duty after a quick change over to start our week of morning shift, so we finished at 10.00p.m. to return at 6.00a.m. We were put on the same beat to cover the surrounding areas of the divisional town headquarters in the same Bedford van and, to complete our inquiries into what had now been christened `the cock end inquiry`. Details of such incidents always spread quickly throughout the force and, particularly throughout the hospital, it was inevitable that the jokes would be forthcoming and sympathy and understanding would be at the back of the queue, but at this time and date we didn't know when the amputation occurred or how when or where and , so our first port of call was the hospital. We chose to go early knowing that the patients were usually awakened at 6.00a.m. and that we would be able to see the patient prior to the doctor's round.

We went to see the Ward Sister prior to going to have a chat to the patient, it was a different Sister to the previous night but, she was expecting us anyway. We inquired as to the medical state of the patient and asked if we were going to be able to talk to him. She immediately told us that he was obviously soar and had been awake for the majority of he night. She went on to say that his wife had been with him until about 4.00.a.m., but hadn't been able to get much sense out of him because of the sedation and, her brother had picked her up and taken her home.

The Sister was quite a comic in her own right by the way she was dealing with the unusual injury sustained and not by being flippant was she funny, but by being matter of fact with her quips, such as, "That's the end to a great relationship.". "He must have seen the end coming.". "Will he now be able to ride the distance?". "I wonder if he'll be embarrassed by the size?". We then asked her if we could interview him, telling her that our concern was the answer to the question as to whether or not someone else was responsible for the amputation and, basically what was the cause. To date he had not given any explanation to anyone.

The Sister then told us that he was out of bed, but that he would find it terribly difficult to walk to the consultancy room, so it was a matter of speaking to him in the ward. As it happened, the ward he was in was a side ward with three beds in it, so privacy was taken care of anyway.

The Sister took us to the ward that the patient was in and introduced us, albeit that it was quite obvious who we were by virtue of the uniforms that we were wearing.

"Hello.", I said, "How are you feeling this morning (as if I couldn't imagine - in pain - in shock - bewildered - depressed and, wondering what life lay ahead for him) we're here just to ask you a few questions, are you okay for us to stay and ask you those questions?". To which he nodded and answered, "Yes.". He was certainly looking forlorn and, from his delivery I was sure that he would have preferred us not to have been there, but he had agreed to answer the questions that we required to be answered.

Nigel then came to life and asked the question, "You came to the hospital in your van, who brought you here?". "I came by myself.", he replied and he continued, "I don't know how the hell I got here."

"Where did you have your accident?" he was asked, only to receive the reply, "In the van!".

I chirped in and asked, "How the hell could that damage be caused in your van, who else was with you?". "No-one.", he replied, I was on me own. I've just been f---ing stupid. Me wife's been here nearly all night asking me what's happened and I've pretended to be asleep or not able to understand what she's saying, but she's got to know some time, hasn't she?. "Yes", I said, "The truth of what happened is going to be told at some time, so let's cut the agrow and tell us how you came about walking into this hospital with half your prick in situe and the other half in your hand?".

He then seemed to get the message that eventually all was going to be revealed, we were wanting to know if there was a third party involved and, if there was, had we got a serious assault incident to investigate?".

He then went into a `couldn't care less mode` saying, "What the f---, let's get it over with, every things finished, I'll tell you what's gone on. There's no-one else, it's just me.

"Well come on, tell us what has happened?", I said.

"I use me van for doing the odd-jobs that I do, it's mostly building work, that I do. The van's old and rattles and vibrates and the engine isn't too good and it runs irregularly. It's age and it wants a good service or it wants to go on the scrap heap", he said. Nigel then interrupted, "Yes, we know what you mean we've driven here in a similar vehicle, an old Bedford with a three gear column change and, although it's serviced regularly it's ready for the scrap heap". I thought, we're not here to compare vehicles, but to get to the bottom of what had happened, so I said, "What's the condition of the van got to do with what's happened?". The patient looked at me and said, "When the van was shaking when I was driving it I used to get excited.". "How do you mean excited?", Nigel said.

It could be seen that the interviewee was drawing things out as if he didn't want to get to the crux of the matter, so I asked, "When you got excited, what happened?". He then continued, "Well, it made me get a hard on, but I couldn't come because I couldn't w--- meself off when I was driving, but there was a piece of wire coming from where the hand break is and, I put it round me cock and, it did the trick when I've done it before, it made me come because it was shaking with the van.".

"Did you put the piece of wire around your cock yesterday?", I enquired. "Yes", came the answer, "I put it round when I was driving up Church Street towards the traffic lights." Nigel then asked, "Did you have your cock out of your trousers?". "Yes, no-one could see and, the van was shaking like hell, so I was getting really worked up."

"So tell us what happened then?", I said. "I was coming up to the traffic lights and they were on green so I went to go straight through, but they changed all of a sudden and, I braked. The foot break isn't very good so I use the hand break as well and, the wire pulled tight and I felt a terrific sting. That was it, it cut it off and it was on the edge of the seat between me legs, just hanging on by a little bit of skin. I had to hide me cock in me pants, I just pulled the wire and it was off." "What, you mean you finished the job by cutting it completely off with the wire?", asked Nigel. The patient then said, "Well, it was hardly on and, it was bleeding like hell. I just put it on the passenger's seat and drove straight to the hospital. What else could I do, but come here to get seen to and, to try and get it put back.".

He had obviously invented the idea of mechanical masturbation, but on this occasion he had somehow tied a slip-knot on the wire, which had then caused a cheese-wire amputation when he pulled the hand break on. I said, "From what we're told, there was no-way it could be stitched back on.", and I couldn't resist saying, "so it's left you a little short for the future.". I then asked the question, "Are you sure there was no-one else involved?". He replied, "There was no-one else at all, it was just me. What am I going to tell the wife?, she's bound to think someone's attacked me for being with someone else, like you did at first. Will you go and tell her that I haven't been unfaithful, because I haven't.".

The request sounded so pathetic and, it was obvious that he was at a `rock bottom` state of self esteem and, required some help, albeit that we had to again check the van first and, the wire which had been the instrument of section, to see if everything matched up. I just then said, "Well, we've a couple of things to do and check out and, if all appears to be as you have said, then that's an end to our inquiries. As a matter of course we will have to see your wife and, as a matter of courtesy tell her that we have no further inquiries to make and, leave it at that, but if you want us to tell her what exactly happened, then we will.". "I want you to tell her, then I wont be forced to tell her, because I know it'll be the end, I know I've been daft and stupid, but I just want her to know that I've never been unfaithful, just tell her please.". "Yes, we will, if that's what you want. We don't have to see you again if our couple of inquires prove to be as we think they will be, so we hope you recover soon and, that things sort themselves out", I said.

We only had one inquiry or matter to attend to and, that was to examine his vehicle and, in particular the hand break and any wire that may be present near by.

As we were leaving the ward we paid the usual courtesy to the ward Sister in her office to enlighten her of our conversation with her patient and, to tell her that we were almost certain that we would not be returning to see him again. We also mentioned that he had asked us to tell his wife what had happened so that she and her staff would be prepared for any problems after she was of knowledge of the facts.

We then went back to the station and, we parked the police van at the side of the impounded vehicle... It was a job to know which of the two vehicles should enter the scrap yard first. The vehicle was still as it had been found and, we opened the doors and, there attached to some mechanism under the hand break was the instrument of excitement, torture and amputation. We saw that at the end of the wire was a slip-knot almost completely closed and, there sure enough were fragments of skin, undoubtedly foreskin, around the knotted end with blood everywhere. It was a positive answer to the cause of the amputation.

We telephoned the ward Sister from the police station to confirm that we wouldn't be back to see her patient as we had confirmed his story and we were convinced that there was no third party involved and therefore no offense committed, to which she quipped, "Well, you now seem to be as detached from the scene as the end of his cock.". There was no answer to that, other than to contemplate the necessity to see his wife and, explain the situation to her, in the kindest way possible. The Sister had also told us that he was likely to remain in hospital for at least another week, so that would give a time gap for all wounds to heal a bit, both pain and family wise.

We went off to the family home and the patient's wife was there with her mother in law and the children and her best friend who lived near-by. It was a case of seeing her on her own, but she insisted that her friend came with her into the front room. She had told her friend about the injury caused to her husband in any event, so it was her wish to know the outcome of the inquiries and, for her friend to hear. Grandma was looking after the kids, she obviously asked how her son was and, we told her that he was better than the previous day, but that he was going to be in hospital for about a week.

All four of us, me and Nigel and the wife together with her friend went into the front room, the door was shut and we all sat down. "You obviously know now what injury your husband has, you've been to the hospital, but you don't know what's happened to cause the injury. We've now found out what did happen and, it's all a bit bizarre, we've just come to tell you as a matter of courtesy that our inquiries are completed and there won't be any further police involvement. Your husband did ask us to tell you that no-one else was involved and asked us to tell you what exactly did happen, but we'll only do that if you want us to. "Yes, tell me. I just want to know. He wouldn't say anything last night, but he obviously was in pain, just tell me.".

I then told her exactly what he had told us, her friend said nothing and, she just sat there in a state of unbelief. I went on to tell her that he was adamant that he had not had any affair and, that he hoped she believed him. She then burst out crying saying, "For God's sake, we've been married for God knows how many years, we've got two kids, why does he have to play with himself like that, he's always got what he wants and, we've always been happy.". She then became totally hysterical and, I was pleased that her friend was present, she burst out into an outrage of abuse towards him, "What have I been, some sex thing, something to use, those kids outside. I don't believe him, he's had someone else. It's over, it's gone, everyone in the hospital knows' I'm not going there again, it's finished. How could he do it to me?"

It was now a domestic and, very sad, from a perfect together family life, it developed into a disorientated mess, because of the situation that the postman and odd job-man had left himself in, there was no answer to that and, up to him to sort out and survive if he could. Without being un-thoughtful or callous I never did find out the outcome and never inquired, but my last wish was to wish them well, but I have always been doubtful of the outcome ever being a 'happy family again', because of the "cheese wire amputation"..

AN UNEXPECTED TRANSFER.

I only had fourteen months experience and, I was called into the Superintendent's office. What for, I didn't know, was it perhaps the sack in my probationary two years?". With some trepidation, I entered the Admin section of the divisional headquarters and, said to the Sergeant in the office, "I've been told that the Super wants to see me, do I make an appointment or do I see him now?". "He'll see you now", he said, "I'll just tell him you're here.". The Sergeant left his office only to return to say to me, "Come through here." I followed him and he knocked on the door and, I heard the Super reply to the knock, "Come in.".

I followed the Sergeant into the office and gave the customary salute to the Superintendent and, the Sergeant then said to him, "Am I alright to leave him with you Sir?", to which he replied "No, you can stay because he'll want kitting out anyway.". I was thinking, what the hell's happening, kitting out for what?, my mind was working overtime.

The Superintendent then said, "I know you've only been here a short time, but it's been noticed that you're doing quite well. We are short of a constable in the C.I.D. at present because of illness and we need a replacement, and you're going to replace him in the short term although you are still in your probationary period, so I want you to do your best and prove my choice right in this particularly busy holiday season. Right you'll be starting in the department tomorrow and, the Sergeant will kit you out and explain the rest to you.". I was almost speechless, but managed to say, "Thank you Sir, I'll do my best.", to which he replied, "I'm sure you will.".

On leaving the Superintendent's office I followed the Sergeant to his office where he told me to sit down while he got my file. He returned and said, "Well, you're the youngest I've ever known to get a spell as a Detective Constable.". The word `Detective` just echoed in my ears, a real life detective, so soon. "Right", the Sergeant said, "What size hat do you take?". "Six and seven eighths, Serg", I replied. It then struck me what the kitting out was all about, a C.I.D. officer was not allowed to leave the station without wearing a trilby and, the force had a delivery of "trilbies" every year from Christies (an established and very well known hat makers) and, that was the kitting out procedure. C.I.D. officers also had a different shaped notebook to fit into the inside pocket of their suits, so once I had signed for my trilby and pocket book, pocket books all being numbered, I was instructed to attend at the C.I.D. office at 9.00a.m. the following morning.

The C.I. D. office was in the divisional headquarters' building and housed the Detective Inspector who was responsible for the divisional crime reported and the supervision of two sub-divisions, a Detective Sergeant and four Detective Constables, the two sub-divisions had two Detective Constables each. It could be looked at as being a bonus to start at 9.00a.m. each day, but the duty could be split or you could be called out at anytime, that being the case the hours could be long without any additional pay, but it was the dream of being a Detective that over-shadowed the downfalls, so let duty commence.

At that time there were no scene of crime officers and, the detective visiting a scene was responsible for searching for evidence, dusting for prints and, photographing them, so I was a "Jack of all Trades" over night. The challenge was there to be concurred.

I went back to my digs that evening after finishing my shift at 10.00p.m. and, sure enough it happened that the other four officers sharing the same digs were sat around the dining room where `Ma` and her husband were. `Ma`, as we all called her, had put on the table some nibbles for us all to tuck into, needless to say the news had spread and, they therefore all new that I had been posted to the C.I.D. They also saw that I was walking in with my trilby, which would you believe was in a Christies' bag and, the ribbing I got was beyond belief. I was beginning to wish that I hadn't been transferred, but the glasses came out and some of Ma's home made beer and wine appeared and, the `piss taking` became less of a problem.

The night then drew to a close and we were all off to bed. I shared a room with a mate named Graham, so it was a matter of getting into my bed and just saying, "When the Super called me in I thought it was for the sack, not a transfer to the C.I.D.". "Bloody hell", said Graham, "How the hell have you landed that?". "I don't know", I replied, "It came out of the blue, I'm going to feel a right prat walking to the station tomorrow wearing my suit and trilby." To which he replied, "We'll all be standing on the doorstep to give you a bit of support.". "Thanks.", I said, and turned over to go to sleep.

The elation, the expectancy and, the unknown, did not help the sleep pattern, but as night follows day, morning follows night and, I was up at six pressing my suit, choosing my shirt and tie and, secretly trying on my trilby to see which tilt suited best. Ma was always up early cooking the regular good English breakfast and, she was quite amused at the hat modeling which was taking place in the dining room with the use of the mirror, which was next to the kitchen where she was usually entrapped with so many hungry mouths to feed.

With the suit, the shirt and, the tie pressed to perfection and, having perfected the trilby tilt, I went back to my bedroom, bathed (there was no shower), dressed and without my jacket and trilby ventured down for breakfast. The lads were there, breakfast was presented as usual for us all to tuck into and, then started the sarcasm. Sherlock Holmes was mentioned so many times, I was offered a brolly when it was mid-summer, but it was said that it was only for show with the quip that I could hold the trilby down with the brolly should the breeze be too strong. It was all good banter and, I left to finish getting ready for work wishing that they all hadn't been present at the same time "taking the piss".

All was ready and, I ventured down the stairs suitably attired, to walk to the police station to start my first period of duty as a Detective. I had my new pocket book in my suit pocket and, my trilby, held in my hand by the front indentations to lift to my head at the appropriate moment, as expected, the whole house were at the front door to see me commence my journey and, at that time they were all quite quiet, but after having gone down the road towards the station I put my trilby on and, there was then the biggest shout that you could ever hear. It was an automatic reaction on hearing the cheer that I turned, lifted my hat and bowed and again turned to continue my journey, amongst the cheers from the doorstep of the digs.

On arriving at the station I signed on duty, which was different, because the C.I.D. had their own signing on book and, who should be there but the Detective Inspector who said, "I'll see you up in my office as soon as you've finished down here.". "Yes Sir, " I said, not knowing what to expect.

I signed on duty and, at the side of the signing on desk were post boxes for the officers in the C.I.D., and one of them now had my name on it. It was my first morning and there were already three messages deposited, one memo was to inform me of the new allowances that I was entitled to, namely clothing allowance, out of pocket expenses (which meant treating genuine informants after information had led to a conviction - at this point in time I didn't have any informants, so this allowance didn't matter), the second was my duty rota and the third memo was to tell me that I now wouldn't be getting my torch and boot allowance following the transfer of duties. It meant therefore that monetary wise I gained nothing, financially everything evened out, but I did gain a trilby.

I ventured up-stairs after having read "my post" and, walked into the office which was that of the Detective Sergeant, whose desk was at the far end of the room and, that of the Detective Constables whose desks were at the other end of the room. The Sergeant got to his feet on me entering the room, he was a man mountain of a man, but when I had briefly been in his company previously I had always got on with him, and he said, "The boss'll see you first, so we'll go through. At the same time as I was walking through the other two Detective Constables, Pete and Rich, echoed welcoming verbal statements, both of them indicating that I shouldn't be too long in the bosses office because they'd sorted out enough work to keep me occupied for some considerable time.

We went through the small corridor and the Sergeant knocked on the D.I.'s door, which was answered with the beckoning call, "Come in.". The D.I. shook my hand and welcomed me to the department, it was strange really, because I had been brought up, in fact born and bread, a matter of doors away from the home of his father and mother in law, the birth place of his wife and he had known my family for many years and of my existence since I was born. That was while living in the town of the police headquarters and, obviously it was known that the family, "down the back" had a member of the family who was a high ranking detective, so all should be careful and watch what they were doing. "Down the back" being a phrase used because all of the houses had a back way to them. There was definitely no nepotism attached to my appointment, because I must have only seen him on three occasion prior to being stationed in the same division as him, which was as of now.

"Welcome to the Department, you know that we are particularly busy at this time of the year, it being summer and, that we have been short staffed for quite sometime, so you are here to help us out and to try and clear up as many crimes as you can. It means you working on your own quite a bit, but you've always got everyone here to fall back on, should you need us, we'll be seeing your reports anyway." he said and, went on to say, "The Sergeant will take you through and show you your desk and introduce you to the other two lads, but you know them anyway I suppose.".

Me and the Sergeant then went through to the office of the D.S. and the D.C's, I was shown my desk and, then a general conversation took place about what crime was being committed In the Division as a whole and, what they were going to pass onto me. There were something of about twelve crime reports that required to be investigated above patrol officer level that were then passed to me with the details contained in seperate folders. The Sergeant then took over saying, "You've got twelve files at the moment. You'll also have to investigate matters that have occurred the previous day and overnight and, you'll learn about that work load when you sign on duty in the morning, so we'll leave you to it to get to know the few files that you've got at the moment.".

That was my induction into the Department. It was now up to me to do the business, that being my best. It was up to me to read the files, inquire about the crime scene day to day as to what had been reported, liaise with colleagues and, get results. Where would I begin?. Too many questions asked might highlight inexperience, incompetence or insecurity, which I was determent not to show, so it was a matter of getting on with the task before me and, resorting to assistance and advice after going as far as I could on any inquiry myself.

It was now going to be a reading and consideration situation for two or three days to get up to speed on the files that I had been given, place them in order of importance and investigate them accordingly

You could never as such investigate every crime individually, because there were too many of them and therefore every crime allocated had to be given time, with the considered most important taking preference to attract the investigating officer's attention.

THE SERIAL INDECENCY MERCHANT

After having read through the files, there were a bank of indecency offenses that stood out, because the crimes were similar, getting progressively worse and, concerned indecent assaults against females, they had occurred within our County and the two adjacent Counties and, they had been occurring for a period of some eight to nine months.

The females attacked were of no particular age, they were just women going about their every day business, walking along any street or footpath, it just seemed that the attacks were against any of those females that took the offender's eye.

However, it was evident that whoever was committing the indecency offenses was progressing into committing indecent acts coupled with force, threats and, violence which was progressing in severity, so I coupled them all together and, asked the adjoining forces to send me details of the offenses committed in their areas, which they did. In total there were twenty eight offenses that could be coupled together as the same person being responsible by way of `Modus Operandi` (Similar methods or techniques of committing offences). The description of the culprit was also similar in virtually all of the incidents.

The description was, a white male, about 30-32 years of age, fair hair, clean shaven, wearing rimless glasses 5' 9" in height, and somewhat rotund in build and usually wearing an open necked shirt and if the weather was inclement he wore a wind-cheater. He was said to speak sharply but softly. He had on a few occasions been seen to run off and jump in a white van which had been parked some distance away from the scene. The van had been seen by victims in all three counties where offenses had been reported, so it was a considered guess that the male person responsible traveled about by virtue of his employment or to specifically commit the offenses.

I then put a circular out to all divisions and sub-divisions and to the adjoining forces stating the type of offences, the description of the suspect and, explaining how the offenses had progressed from being an incident assault where the assailant had run up to the victim(s) and grabbed hold of the victim(s) crutch or breast(s), to where he was going behind the females and putting his arm around their necks and saying, "Don't move" or "Keep still and, the time he was taking to commit the offenses was increasing. The initial offenses were reported to have been committed in vicinities where there were or could be expected to be a number of people present and then for him to run away and, the recent offenses committed were in more remote areas and the assaults were becoming more intense by clothing being ripped and the groping more vicious and threatening.

After having circulated the details, the Crime Intelligence Officer for the division contacted me and, then told me that he had been collating information from the uniform information sheets only to find that over the previous eleven or twelve months there had been a number of indecent exposures reported where the description was the same as that being given for the person responsible for the indecent assaults. Indecent exposure offenses were recorded, statistically as misdemeanors and not crimes, so had not shown up on crime reports and ultimately on crime statistics, but by description the "Fat Flasher", as he had become known was the one and same person as the indecency merchant.

Together with the Crime Intelligence Officer, all the information was collated and, "our little rotund bespectacled offender" seemed to have started his evil ways by adorning a mackintosh and then walking towards females and pulling his mackintosh open, thereby exposing his private parts. He was obviously excited on those occasions because his penis was always reported to have been erect.

There was then another report of an indecent assault reported and, the uniform department had attended at the scene. The assailant had walked towards the young lady victim as she was walking through a park area, after having her pack-up lunch in the park and, she was just on her way back to work, when the assault occurred. The assailant walked past her and then turned around and, grabbed the young woman around the neck while holding a knife in the same hand and, saying "If you move, I'll f---ing kill you". At the same time the assailant was grabbing at her crutch and breasts.

The young woman was obviously terrified and, she was quite surprised when the assailant let go of her and ran off. The description given by the victim was once again the same as that given by previous victims.

The reported crime was put down to me to investigate with the others previously reported and I again circulated the details of the assault and the description of the assailant within the force and to the local newspapers in all three counties where the offenses had been reported, sadly no useful information was forthcoming to identify the person responsible for these now serious crimes. What was it going to develop into?, was the question to be asked and, there was no answer to that without the culprit being caught.

At this time the force and other forces had started to use `Photofits`, which was a picture of an individual which was made up from prepared part drawings of the anatomy which were placed together at the direction of the witness giving the description until, the witness was eventually satisfied that the end product, that being the completed form or picture of the individual was as near as could be attained. I therefore decided to have a photfit of the suspect prepared by the one officer in the county force that had been trained to interview the witnesses and prepare the end product, that being an image as near to the looks of the person wanted as there could be.

I really, at this time, had no confidence in the use of photofits and, was never an advocate in the use of them. Despite my lack of confidence in photo fits arrangements were made for two of the females who seemed to have given the best descriptions, to be seen for them to place together the various drawings of parts of a face which best resembled the features of the individual to arrive at a final image.

The trained officer saw both witnesses separately and, sat down with both of them for some considerable time and, arrived consequently with two photo fits. It was amazing to see how similar they both were. The two victims were then seen by me and the officer who had prepared them and, we showed them their own photo fit and the other, then together they made one or two alterations to one of the photfits and came up with an end product which was as near as they both could say was as near to the assailant as possible.

I had a photographs taken of the agreed photfit and, these were circulated to all officers and to the press. I also contacted the regional television news desks and gave them the story together with a copy of the photographed photfit. The following day and evening the papers and both television channels covered the story and showed in print and on television the image prepared from the description of the witnesses of the assailant. I was `chuffed` that I had pieced together the crimes that had and were being committed and, that it was receiving the high profile reporting that it was.

I was `chuffed` only until the following morning when I signed on duty at the same time as the Detective Inspector who beckoned me to his office to have a word with me, about what I knew not, but I was soon to find out when the door of his office was closed which left just me and him there. "Who the hell gave you permission to give the story of the indecent assaults to the press and T.V.?", he blurted. "No-one", I said. "Do you know that if anything is given out to the press and in particular T.V., then it is me who sanctions it and it is me who gives the story and the interview if there is to be one, not you. I'm expecting the Hierarchy to be in touch later to question me about the release and, if they do then you'll be back in bloody uniform straight away", he ranted. I said I'd done it with best of intention and hoped that we'd get the necessary result from the publicity. "Right, get get on with what you're doing and, if there are any repercussions I'll be seeing you again", he said. I left his office not knowing if I was punched or counter sunk, my spirit certainly was!.

There was no response to the publicity that day, so my days duty was miserable following the bollacking and, the down feeling went home with me and added to that was a somewhat sleepless night. On waking up the following morning, after little sleep, I got ready for work and went down for breakfast. There were two of the lads there and the landlord and Ma doing the cooking and, they all knew that I was investigating the indecency jobs, sure enough that had to be the topic of conversation with the landlord saying, "By, you got some coverage last night in the papers and on tele on that job you're on". "Yes", I said, "so I believe, I didn't see the tele coverage, but there was plenty in the press. We'll have to see what happens now". I couldn't wait to get away from the breakfast table.

Having left the table I finished my ablutions and gathered necessities to leave the digs and meander my way to the office in the hope that I wasn't going to sign on duty at the same time as the boss.

The morning past routinely by visiting a couple of scenes of crime and, I returned to the office at lunch time. A message had been left for me to telephone a police officer of a neighbouring force about the indecent assaults. My natural reaction was to question it and ask myself, "What the bloody hell now?". It could be anything and, the officer who had asked me to telephone him was stationed some thirty miles away.

With some trepidation I telephoned the officer who had called, I told him who I was and said that I was returning his call. He said, "I've got some good news for you. There's a fellow in here who has called in with his wife to give himself up for having committed the indecent assaults." If this was the case then I couldn't believe my luck, because I wanted to show that what I had done publicity wise had proved right, albeit that I hadn't adhered to the correct procedure, and that I was certain in my own mind if this assailant was allowed to continue at large, then we would be soon investigating an offense of rape or something more serious.

I then said, "We'll be over to interview him as soon as we can get there". The officer replied, "Hang on, that's not all, he's identical to the photfit". I said, "It can't be that good!". "Well, you can take

77

it from me that it is, it's bloody well identical", he replied, only to continue, "Apparently he was at home with his Mrs. this evening when the paper was delivered, his wife was reading it and saw the photo fit and turned to him, showed him it and said it looked like him and, then she just chuckled and read on".

I said,"You're joking, it literally can't be that good". "It is", he went on, "You just haven't heard it all yet. After his wife had said that, the Minister from the church telephoned them and jokingly said that he had seen his picture on television. It was after the Minister had telephoned him that he told his wife that it was him who had been responsible for the assaults on the women. Apparently they are a God fearing couple and, after talking about it decided that he should give himself up and go to the police station, which he has done and, he's waiting for you to pick him up". I told him that we would be on our way as soon as was possible to pick him up.

I then spoke to the Detective Sergeant and put him in the picture and said if it was alright I'd take the C.I.D. van to collect the self confessed assailant and bring him back to the divisional headquarters for questioning. That was agreed and, me and one of the other Detective Constables set off to collect the prisoner.

We got to the police station where he was being held and, the officer I had been speaking to was awaiting our arrival. My colleague and I introduced ourselves and, as per custom we were invited to the canteen to discuss the happenings of the day, only to hear that on being asked if he wanted a solicitor contacting, he had replied, "No, thank you, but I would like to speak to the Minister and, I'd like him to come and see me if that's possible". "We arranged for the Minister to be telephoned and then he spoke to him and told him everything." said the officer. "The Minister came, He's with him now talking to him and his wife. It's a really strange situation, because after I first saw him I gave him a pen and paper to write down what he could remember and, between then and the Minister attending he's written four pages of incidents that he can remember and, here they are", continued the officer. He then handed to me the written notes.

I then asked if we could see him, because in his notes he now admitted some fifty eight offences, from indecent exposure to serious indecent assaults coupled with threats to kill.

I said, "I can't believe that he can remember them all, to which the officer replied, "He just couldn't stop talking and writing, but I think he's come to the end now. That'll improve your figures! (meaning detected crimes cleared up)".

We then went down into the cell block and into the interview room and the detective officer went off to collect and bring to us the bespectacled, rotund prisoner and, in front of me I had a copy of the photo fit picture which was identical to the man who entered the interview room, I was absolutely amazed, in fact speechless, it could not have been batter had it been an actual photograph of him.

The officer introduced us, and said, "I'll leave you to it, but if you want anything give us a shout", we thanked him and he left.

I said, "I understand that you have surrendered yourself, given yourself up, for committing a number of offenses of indecency against women, is that right?".

He replied, "Yes", without any hesitation.

It is quite surprising that when such matters are reported in the media that a man has been arrested for committing indecent assaults in particular areas that other victims will come forward, who have not wanted to come forward previously for fear of being disbelieved or because of embarrassment and, they report having been assaulted. The late reports are all usually perfectly genuine. It was with this in mind that I said to him, showing him the sheets of paper that the officer had handed to me, "Is this your handwriting?". He replied, "Yes". I continued, "Are there any more offenses that you have committed that you want to tell us about?".

He thought for a while and said, "No. I can't remember any more. It's been difficult remembering them that I have told you about because when I've done it I try to forget it, but if I do remember any more I'll tell you about them. I've told my wife everything and the Minister and my wife is going to stand by me".

My colleague then said, "We're taking you back to our police station now and, we will be further interviewing you there, so we've got about half an hours journey and you can be thinking on the way. We're going to take you into the charge room now and they will release you to our custody. We will also see your wife and explain to her what is happening". We then took him to the charge room, my colleague stayed with him and I went to see his wife to explain.

His wife was in one of the interview rooms being comforted by the Minister, she was sobbing with disbelief saying, "I can't believe it's happening. No matter what he's done, I still love him and want to be with him". I told her that he would be with us for some time and that we were taking him to our police station and that we would keep her in touch with what was happening. They had been married for about eight years and, there were no children, she didn't want her mum and dad to know or any other member of the family, but she was in the safe hands of the Minister who assured us that she would be cared for and, that he was taking her back to his home to be further comforted by him and his wife and children. I took his details and telephone number to contact him and the prisoner's wife and, told him that I would undoubtedly want to see him again, because of his involvement. He then said, "I'm told by the family to tell you everything, as they have said they will, because they want everything cleared up. They both appreciate how serious the matter is". I left them telling them that I would be in touch.

Everything was coming together and, albeit it was an `easy cop` by virtue of him giving himself up, a lot of ground work had been done before and, I hadn't forgotten the bollocking I had received for not getting permission to make public the offenses that had been committed and in particular the publication of the photfit.

We were ready to return to the station, we said our good-byes' to the officers who had assisted us and, made arrangements for the necessary statements concerning the incident to be forwarded to us. We left the charge room and walked to our Morris Minor van and, of course the prisoner was allocated the make shift seat in the back of the vehicle which had been stabalised as best that it could be. We were on our way.

During the journey the self confessed perpetrator of the crimes couldn't stop talking, he was appreciating the support of his wife and the church and, saying how pleased he was that everything now would be out in the open, that he and his wife could start afresh, that they could have the family that they always wanted. We reminded him that there was some way to go before everything was going to be finished, but in general he was happy that his conscience was going to be cleared by virtue of his admissions. He also showed some remorse for his victims and said that he had asked the Minister to pray for them, and the Minister said that he would. Without being sceptical, I wondered how many victims would want him or the Minister to say prayers for them.

The journey being over, we parked the van and, walked into the charge room with the prisoner and, I explained the circumstances of the arrest to the Duty Sergeant and, that we wanted the prisoner lodged in the cells until we had collated all the information that we wanted from adjoining police areas and our own reports and that we wanted him lodged in the cells overnight until we had all the information necessary so that we could further interview him. The Duty Sergeant accepted the circumstances and the prisoner was detained in custody until further inquiries were made, so he was lodged in the cells overnight, to be seen in the morning.

Who should be in the charge room at the time of our entry and, at the time of me giving the explanation of the arrest and number of offenses admitted, was the Detective Inspector, the very person who had castigated me for depriving him of his appearance before the press and T.V. After the prisoner was `put to bed` for the night I was making my way to my desk to arrange my tomorrows programme, the time was about half past eleven, there was present in the office the Detective Sergeant and the two detective Constables I worked with, one of whom had been with me to collect the prisoner and, out of his office came the Detective Inspector.

"Well, you say he's admitted fifty odd offenses, that'll make our figures good this month, you've done a bloody good job, I'll be able to tell the hierarchy tomorrow and they'll be dead chuffed. I'm off home now. I'll see you in the morning" and, off went the Detective

Inspector to his bed. There was no withdrawal of the reprisal I had had and, no recognition of the worry it had caused me, but an understanding by me that many lesson can be learned in life by there being certain senior officers being afraid `of their own arses` and, he was certainly one.

As it does, the following day arrived, I was elated at the arrest, but now all the information had to be placed together, all the crime reports scrutinized with the admissions married to them and, any admissions not reported, investigated as best that they could be. Overnight, in my absence, the night duty officers had circulated the arrest with the request that any further information and reports be forwarded to us. Having circulated the admissions there were no-more forthcoming, but there was confirmation that their crime reports would be sent to us.

It was now a matter of getting him before the Court and it was a matter of him being charged with an offence to either hold him in custody, or for him to be remanded on bail to a future date to appear before the Court. All the papers were collated as far as could be, to be presented to the Court and, the prisoner was charged with two holding charges which were considered to be the most serious and, because of the admissions the other offenses would eventually be listed and put to the accused when he appeared before the Court, when he would be asked if he wanted them taken into consideration when he was sentenced. If he agreed to them being taken into consideration then he couldn't be charged with them thereafter and, it would also cause them all to be regarded as detected crimes, thus greatly improving our detection of crime rate.

It was decided to place the accused before the Magistrates' Court the following day, when it was anticipated that all the information would be to hand and he could be dealt with there and then. Consideration had been given to the fact that he was remorseful and, that he had never appeared before a Court previously, so it was firm opinion that he would not get more than six months imprisonment, so the Magistrates could deal with him and not have to commit him to the Quarter Sessions Court, where he could receive a longer sentence. It was also the case that if the Magistrates deemed that he should receive a longer sentence than they could give him, then they could commit him anyway.

All was ready for him to appear before the Court the following day, after there being a great deal of paper work prepared, when the prisoner asked to see me. The thought went through my mind that everything that had been done would have to re-done if there was a change of heart by him or a change of story, so with some trepidation I went to see him with the colleague that I had been working with putting the paper work together.

We saw him in the cell block interview room and, with some hesitation I said, "You wanted to see me?".

"Yes", he replied and then went on, "You know that you asked me to think of anything else that might have happened, well there was another one, I've remembered it, but I didn't know if you would want to know about it". "I want to know about them all", I said.

He then said, "Does it matter if the woman seemed to like it?".

"You just tell us about it and, we'll tell you if it makes any difference", said my colleague. "Well", he said, "I was in my van, driving along this road when I drove over a hump backed bridge. It was a real sunny day and, everyone was walking about without their coats on. As I went over the bridge there was a girl there of about twenty, she was leaning against the bridge side with one of her feet on the bridge side looking into the river. She seemed to turn me on so I turned into a side road and stopped and got out of my van and, walked back to where she was standing. I could see that she hadn't got any tights on and she just had slip on shoes. There were no houses near-by and no-one about so I went and leant against the bridge next to her. She didn't say anything and, all I said was that it was a nice day. She still didn't say anything so I put my hand up her skirt and she didn't move, she just stood there,turned around and looked at me and, she still didn't say anything. I felt the edge of her knickers, they were loose, and I put my fingers inside her and played about,she still didn't move".

I said, "You mean to tell me that you fingered the girl and played about and she still didn't say anything to you?". He said adamantly, "Yes, she did enjoy it because she was all wet and didn't move".

My colleague then said, "What did you do then?", to which he replied' "I just finished and, just walked away to my van and then drove away".

I said to him, "We'll see if anything was reported, but I don't think it will stop us going ahead with the hearing tomorrow and, if it was as you've said' then the odds are that the matter will not have been reported anyway". The necessary enquiries were made and there had been no such report, so because of the circumstances didn't change, it was Court tomorrow.

I went with my colleague back to the cell block to see the prisoner, to tell him that no report had been received about the bridge incident and, that all would be going ahead as planned. Before leaving the prisoner I couldn't resist asking him, "What pleasure did you get from touching these women?".

He replied, "I got a hard on if I saw a woman that I liked and then I used to come".

"Do you mean that you would masturbate when you were indecently exposing yourself and when you were assaulting the women?", I asked.

He then said, When I started doing it I would just come when I showed myself to them. Then when I started to get hold of them, I used to shoot my load straight away, but it was taking longer all the while".

"What you mean is that you used to ejaculate just by touching them and then it was taking longer to ejaculate the more you did it. Is that right?", I asked. To which he replied, "Yes".

I then asked him, "What would you have done if you hadn't ejaculated?"

"I'd have had to keep touching them until I come", he said.

On that note we left the prisoner, but it showed me what a danger the little rotund man was, because basically there was no woman safe to walk the streetswhen he was about. I was convinced in my own mind, that had he not reached full satisfaction himself when committing the offences, that he would have continued with the assault until he had, and if necessary to reach his full satisfaction he would ultimately commit the offense of rape. I had become quite obvious why the offences were getting more serious, because he was no longer getting full satisfaction by merely exposing himself, so he then had to touch the victims to achieve that satisfaction and, it was quite apparent that the assaults were taking longer for him to reach his peak of sexual satisfaction.

At first the assailant had refused to see a solicitor, but he had eventually agreed and, the solicitor wanted to delay matter and have the case adjourned, but he would not hear of it and wanted to have the case finished with, with his solicitor mitigating for him, which he did. The case was duly heard and, on conviction, on his first appearance before the Court, their Worships found the crimes serious enough to sentence him to six months imprisonment, after hearing his solicitor mitigation and hearing of his wife's support and, on hearing the Minister telling them how assistance and help was available to him through the church. I truly believed that that was the last I would see of him.

I was wrong, some five months later, I was asked to stand in for a fellow officer to give a talk to Probation Officers and Volunteer Probation Officer Assistants. The volunteers were people who gave their time and services voluntarily to assist Probation Officers with their work load. I was waiting for the people to settle in the room before starting my talk when I saw a female enter the room who I recognised, but could not immediately place her. She was then followed by a man, her husband, non other than our rotund, bespectacled indecency merchant, who obviously by that time had been released early by virtue of good behaviour. I just could not believe that he was now training to become a volunteer Probation Officer Assistant.

Needless to say the talk did not go ahead and the matter was rectified by asking the question of whether or not the Probation Service had enquired into the background of all their volunteer assistants, to which the answer had to be, "No". I never heard of him thereafter, but I doubt, in my own mind that he would not transgress again.

A SPEIGHT OF BURGLARIES
AND, THE DOCTOR'S WIFE.

It was mid-summer and, the offenses reported were assaults, which happened as a result of drunken brawls, following the holiday maker's brain escape, causing them to drink too much by way of relaxation during the holidays. They were soon investigated and cleared up, because invariably the victim knew the assailant, who was either a member of the family or a close friend who had gone on holiday with them and, the first person to punch when the drink took over. Hardly any of them ever progressed to a Court hearing, but experience was gained in receiving the reports, interviewing people assessing the evidence to present before the Detective Inspector, who at that time was totally responsible for making the decision as to whether or not a matter should be placed before the Court.

There was the inevitable shoplifting, particularly at the M & S and Woolworths Stores and, inevitably the gift shops. I often used to wonder if they took their ill-gotton gains back home to dish out if they weren't caught, to family and friends as presents and, whether or not they had any conscience when they were doing so.

At the same time there always seemed to be a speight of burglaries and, history of burglaries committed during the summer season would seem to indicate that persons responsible were either the migrant summer fair workers or, the local burglars who wanted to lead us to believe that it was the `migrant summer fair workers`, that were the culprits.

It so happened that such a speight of burglaries did occur and, they were worrying, because they were being committed at night and, while the householders were in their beds (At that time burglar alarms and crime prevention aids were hardly heard of). Obviously, all the C.I.D. officers were aware of the burglaries, but at that time they hadn't been allocated to one officer to investigate.

I left the digs on a particularly bright and sunny morning to sign on duty without knowing what was ahead, but I was about to find out when I signed on duty at the same time as the Detective Inspector and the Detective Sergeant. The Sergeant just said, "We'll see you in the boss's office when you've finished down here". I immediately knew that that was for a bollocking (but I couldn't think why, unless I'd gone out without wearing my trilby), or to action some particular investigation or investigations to me. On attending the Detective Inspector's office, I was to find out that it was the latter, there had been some nine burglaries committed in the area during the night, over a period of some four weeks, in good class areas, where the burglar had entered through ground floor windows by force and, then stolen cash or valuables that he could carry with him. It so happened that during the night another one had been committed at a bungalow on the outskirts of the town just on the edge of a wooded area. The break in had been reported by the lady of the house and the uniform officers had attended and, wanted the C.I.D. to take over the investigation. The investigations were then allocated to me and, that of course was what they wanted to see me about.

Again, to my mind it was a case of, give the `Rooky`, the undetectable jobs to deal with and, by doing so they could justify that an effort was being made to detect the crimes reported.

I set about getting the crime reports of the burglaries that had been reported and the details of the one committed over night. They all fitted a similar pattern, detached properties, affluent area, break-in by way of a ground floor window, no disturbance of the occupants and, no regard as to whether they were in the properties or not and, they had all been committed over the previous six weeks. Quite a lot of cash and a considerable amount of jewelery had been taken, even from bedrooms where the occupants had been in bed, which made the offenses particularly serious, so serious that the law described such crimes as aggravated burglaries, therefore questions had to be and were going to be asked about the stage that the investigations had reached. Those questions were going to be asked by the victims and also the hierarchy when the crime figures were produced, it was a matter that even then statistics mattered and, those concerned with producing the statistics were more concerned with figures that the effect crime had on the victim.

Having read the crime reports of all the burglaries and, the report of the overnight burglary I set off in the C.I.D. van to the scene of the crime armed with the fingerprint kit and the forensic attachments together with the photography equipment. I was unable to speak to the uniformed officer who had attended the burglary scene during the night because he had gone off duty, having completed his shift. I was now the one man band after having been given the task of solving the crimes. Albeit I was inexperienced, the determination was there, but there was also a feeling of me wanting to question my every action, possibly that was insecurity because of the inexperience, but I had to get on with it and the `ball was in my court` to do my best and detect the reported crimes, if I could?".

I arrived at the scene of the overnight burglary and, found that the other burglaries were all withing a half mile radius. They were positioned on a road between two towns, which was now quiet because of a by-pass, they were set back from the road within tree lined gardens and a wood at the rear. They were situated on a rise which allowed them to overlook the town and look out onto the sea and the bay. It couldn't be any more of a picturesesque position and ideal location to live in.

I drove the van into the driveway with my equipment in the back, got out and knocked on the door. The door was opened by an extremely attractive female, I introduced myself and explained, after having shown her my warrant card, that I was now the officer in charge of the investigation into the recent burglaries in the area. She invited me in and, it being mid-morning invited me to a coffee and, at the same time explaining that since she had discovered the break in that she was in a state of shock and had taken a libation of brandy to cool her nerves. She asked me if I would join her by partaking of a similar libation in a glass or with my coffee. I declined and, she excused herself for having to partake of a further glass for medicinal purposes and, filled her glass to drink with her coffee as I was drinking my coffee.

We sat down in the lounge with our drinks and, I asked her what had happened, explaining to her at the same time, that the uniformed officer who had attended following her report was now at home and in bed, but that I had read his report together with some other eight reports of similar burglaries in the area. She went on to tell me that she had gone to bed at about ten o'clock the night before and fallen asleep straight away after having a day out shopping with her friends. She then said that she had awakened at about seven o'clock and sat up in bed, put the light on and, realised that her clothes were not where she had left them and, all the drawers in one of the dressing tables were open. The first reaction naturally was to panick, which she did.

She went on to tell me that she pulled herself together a little after having got out of bed and went straight to the living room after having put every light on that she past, albeit that dawn was breaking. I interrupted her and asked, "Who was with you?". "No-one", she replied, "My husband is away, and has been for about ten weeks, he's a doctor and, he goes away for three months at a time on cruises as the ship's doctor. I could go with him, and usually do, but this time I just wanted to stay at home. He'll be home in a few weeks. He was in private practice here for many years, but then he retired, so now he goes on these cruises to keep his hand in and, for a change of scenery. He's quite a lot older than me, but we've been together for the past ten years".

I said, "Well being on your own will obviously make your fear of what has happened more intense and totally unease you, so it's quite understandable that you needed a brandy".

I continued saying, "Well let's have a look at where he or they got in and then we can can follow his or their way around the bungalow, but first have you moved anything or touched anything since you found that you had been broken into?". "No", she said, the policeman told me not to, so I haven't".

The intruder had obviously got in through the utility room window by forcing it with a heavy screw-driver or gemmy and then climbed over the units inside the utility room, to then visit every room in the property, opening every drawer that he came across. I asked the lady if she had checked what was missing, to which she replied, "I haven't, because the policeman told me not to touch anything until you'd been, but I did check to see if my handbag was in the living room where I'd left it and, it isn't, it's gone and, it had quite a bit of money in it, about two hundred pounds".

I then said to her, "I'll just get my equipment out of the van to photograph and fingerprint where the intruder has obviously been and, then we can have another chat and I'll be able then to take a statement from you". To which she replied, "Is it alright for me to get a shower then because I don't think he's been in the bathroom?". I'd already looked in the bathroom and, there was no showing that the burglar had been in there, so I said, "I'm sure it will be alright if you get a shower".

I left the bungalow to go to the C.I.D. van which was parked in the drive to collect my equipment. My knowledge of, forensics and photography, were limited to a beginners course that I had been on, but I was determined to show a professional attitude and approach. Having been to the van I returned to the bungalow laden with two haversacks containing the fingerprint and photographic equipment. Straight away I started examining the scene of the crime from the point of entry, remembering everything that I had been taught, dusting for fingerprints. I had already been outside and there were no footprints to be found, so that was a negative.

The point of entry and the drawers, on examination showed that the intruder hadn't used gloves, there were fingerprints all over the place. They all had to be revealed by dusting and then photographed, which took time and, even more time because of my inexperience, which I was never going to admit to the victim.

Having started the dusting and, having found the fingerprints in the utility room, I was interrupted by the lady of the house, who came in, obviously having had a shower, just as I was about to photograph the sets of prints that I had found. She had a towel wrapped around her and nothing else and, she was asking me again if I wanted a coffee laced with a brandy, I again refused explaining that I had a good deal of work to do, but a nice cold drink would be appreciated, to which she replied, "I'll get you one, will orange do?, to which I answered, "Yes", and within minutes my iced orange arrived. I was there for some three hours dusting for fingerprints and then photographing them and, experiencing the lady of the house dressed in a towel to the minimum of summer wear and, then it was my task to ask her then to check as to what had been stolen (after having completed the examination of the scene).

She walked around the house and said, "I'm going to have to go around the house at my leisure and make a list, but you know that my handbag has gone anyway, so you can put that in my statement and I can let you know if I find anything else that is missing". "Yes", I said, "You take your time in assessing what has gone and, I can always come down and add to your statement".

We then went into the lounge area and, I sat on one of the settees and, she then moved herself from being in front of the fireplace, together with her glass of brandy, to sit on the same settee, but the opposite end. To say the least, I was feeling particularly uncomfortable, but the job in hand was mostly completed, but I still had the statement to take, so I commenced that task and included all the information that I could about the burglary and what had gone missing, but kept being interrupted by the ladies questions of intrigue, about what I did, how I did it, was I married, had I got a girlfriend and, where did I venture to when I went out. I replied in the most polite way, that I was engaged and due to get married and, that it was my task now to find the burglar, then saying to her, "I'll have to get back now to get the photographs printed and the fingerprints checked, the finger prints are not only checked for person in our area, but also in the Merseyside area, the Manchester and Birmingham areas and also in the London area, there are some good prints so we'll have to wait and see what the check reveals". As I was leaving I had the feeling that she wanted me to stay for ever, but I resisted the temptation, saying, "If there is anything else that you find to be missing then telephone us and, if there is any progress in the investigation then I'll be in touch".

I then went back to the vehicle with my equipment and drove off to the station, thankful of getting out of what had become a compromising situation. The thought in my head being that she had been burgled while she was asleep in bed and, betting myself that if she'd awakened while the burglar was in the bedroom that she would have dragged him into bed. Maybe I was wrong, but I don't think so.

On returning to the station the photographs of the prints were developed and, then circulated to all the criminal record offices to be checked against their bank of prints and, then it was a matter of waiting for the outcome of the checks and, at the same time making inquiries locally and amongst the fairground personnel. The inquiries locally and at the fair ground didn't bear any result, so in the meantime I had visited all the other scenes of the burglaries that were similar and, was positive in my own mind that it was one and the same person, so I contacted all the criminal record offices where the prints for checking had been sent to and asked them to be collated and checked to see if there was a match. Now, it was a wait and see case with regards to the prints, they usually took some two to three weeks to let us have a result whether it be negative or positive.

My work was not done at the bungalow of the last reported break-in, because the doctor's wife left a message for me every morning, to say that she was still checking as to what had been taken and that she had found something else that had gone missing and wanted to add to her statement and could I call round for her to tell me. Dutifully I attended to add to the statement, only to find the lady of the house, in mid morning, seductively dressed just having got out of the shower or sitting in the sun with the intention of the sun being able to tan virtually every part of her body. These updated reports of what had gone missing were awaiting me at the office for the following five or six days, as you can imagine, the lads in the office were taking the micky and, I was having to attend wishing that the doctor's cruise had come to an end now or certainly soon.

A week had passed and I'd been summoned to the dwelling for an update on each and every morning, with the smallest of mention of what else she had found missing, but only to entice me to partake of a drink while adding to her statement while she was there adding to her tan whilst lounging on a sun-bed facing south with the sun blazing down. After having added to the statement I was able to tell her on the fifth day that I was going away the following day to stay on the east coast, at a lovely seaside venue, to put the finishing touches to my marriage arrangements. That didn't even stop her wanting to engage me in an unwanted relationship, which by this time was so obvious, when she said as I was leaving, "As soon as you're back come and see me, he wont be back then and it will be nice for you to tell me how you've got on and enjoyed your holiday".

I couldn't wait to get out of the house, which I did, saying to her that I would have her informed of the results of the fingerprint checks as soon as they were to hand and, that if I wasn't able to convey the results of the fingerprint tests to her then someone else would cause her to be so informed.

I went off on holiday to stay with my girlfriend's family and, during the stay all necessary arrangements were made for the forthcoming marriage which would take place some twelve weeks later at a church in my girlfriend's home town, arrangements had been made for my family and friends for them to travel and stay at various hostelries over the wedding week-end and hopefully for everything to run smoothly.

I had known my girlfriend for quite some time, she was a teacher, newly qualified at a college in North Wales, to teach in primary schools and also to teach art. I had searched and agreed a tenancy on a furnished flat, which had a beautiful view over the bay at the front and, a view of the mountains to the back of the property. All now that had to happen was for the marriage to take place without a hitch and, for her then to get a job teaching at one of the schools in the area.

I returned to my desk after my weeks break, only to find that there had been no results forthcoming on the fingerprints taken from the scenes of the the burglaries, but there was a message from the lady victim which was received early on the morning of my return to duty, to ask that I contact her, because she was having difficulty completing the insurance claim and, she had also found a couple of other items now missing (Not specified - end of message).

I later telephoned her and explained the position to her, that there were at present no results from the fingerprint bureaus and, asked her what else was now missing, so that we could circulate the description or descriptions of the possessions to other forces and dealers. She replied that she must complete the insurance claim before her husband returned home and that it was imperative that I went to see her, for her to be able to tell her husband what had happened when he arrived home in about five days time and, for me to advise her of the best way of doing it.

It so happened that the Detective Inspector and the Detective Sergeant had `clocked` the recall from the doctor's wife, immediately on my return to duty, the `piss taking` started, "Have you seen the message from the doctor's wife for you to go down there and see her, she hasn't rung all week when you've been off, I'm sure she wants a visit sooner than later, you better get off now before we get anymore calls, we're sure she'll have the coffee waiting. "Take the van", said the Detective Sergeant, which seemed to please the Detective Inspector by virtue of his smirk and giggle.

It so happened that Nigel, who I was in digs with and, whom I had been on the quarry incident with, was assigned to the C.I.D. for his two weeks probationary training in the C.I.D., so I got hold of him before he was allocated any job and, explained to him that I was investigating the burglaries and gave him all the details apart from the apparent promiscuity of the complainant and, asked him to go and take the additional statement following the telephone call that the complainant had made that morning. I went on to tell him that he could take the C.I.D. van and return as soon as possible for me to be able to circulate what other possessions were missing. In other words, I chickened out of possibly being compromised.

I went to my desk only to find that there was correspondence from the fingerprint bureaus left for me to deal with, after they had forgotten that I had asked them in the department to assist if the results came in. Nothing had been done, they had not seen that there was a match of the fingerprints examined as stated in the correspondence, in other words `they couldn't give a nack` about my work and investigations when I was away, but piled it up for my return. Anyhow, by now Nigel was well on his way to see the doctor's wife and obtain the necessary statement.

There was a match on six of the specimens forwarded for examination. I had never before completed a dusting and gone on to complete the photographic work to enable the check to be made, I was completely elated that I had achieved identifications on the prints and, then the remaining results arrived from the other two bureaus that same day as I returned to duty and that placed the burglar responsible for all eight burglaries that I was placed to investigate, what a success. I decided to tell no-one else in the department at that time the results of the fingerprint tests, firstly because they assigned the burglaries to me to investigate, thinking in their minds that there was no chance of them ever being detected and, secondly because they were `taking the micky`, about the apparent enticement of the doctor's wife. I now had the identity of the burglar, thanks to the fingerprint bureaus and, he was a Liverpudlian who worked at fair grounds and, travelled with them around the country, he was twenty five years old, 5'9", long dark brown hair, slim build, usually unshaven and, with tatoos on his arms depicting naked ladies and on his back a huge tattoo of a hunt, with the hunt following the hounds and the fox disappearing into into the crevasse of his arse with only the bushy tail protruding and leaving to the imagination what they were hunting for. Once found then he should be easily identified.

Nigel returned after a couple of hours with his usual sombre way, telling me that he had taken the statement, but exclaiming that he had been taken aback by being received, when he knocked on the door, by the lady of the house wearing the flimsiest of night attire and, on seeing him had immediately asked where I was. I was not there, thank goodness!.

With the identification details, the fingerprint bureaus had also forwarded photographs of the identified person, now it was a matter of finding him. Nigel didn't know that I knew who was responsible for the burglaries, but I told him that to progress the enquiry we had to check the fairgrounds. We still had the use of the C.I.D. van to travel to the fairgrounds to search for the burglar and, those in the C.I.D. office were busy with other matters so we could get straight off and engage ourselves in the search.

There were five fairground sights in three seaside locations and, the first site proved totally negative. The second site proved to be helpful when answers were received from the stall holders that the named person had worked on the fairground until recently, but had now moved on to another fairground, at a resort in an adjacent police force area. Nigel, by this time was asking me how I knew who was responsible for the crimes, so I had no option but to tell him and, then travel off to the fairground which was set on the seafront in the adjoining police area, which was not far away. If you travelled into another forces area it was courtesy to inform them that you were going onto their patch, but you still had the same authority within any police area immediately adjoined to yours.

Nigel, in his inimitable way questioned the right of venturing into the domain of the neighboring force without telling them, but I quietened him by telling him that while he had been away taking the statement I had telephoned the neighboring force and couldn't get through, which was not unusual during the summer months, so it was a matter of getting on with the job.

We arrived at the fairground and introduced ourselves at the show-ground office, which was a hut and, spoke to a person from the local authority who was managing the ground who had with him at that time two of the ride owners and, that proved to be particularly helpful. We merely asked them if they knew the person we wanted and showed them the photograph, they both looked at it, looked at each other and, in unison said, "Yes". I then asked them if he was still on the site and, one of them said, "Yes. He's only just come here, he's on the waltzers". The other one added, "He always works on the waltzers wherever he goes. I saw him last night so he should still be here".

I thanked them and, drove down the site until we came to the waltzers, there were few people about, so we stopped and walked onto the waltzer ride and went to the cash office where we asked the money taker if the wanted alleged burglar was working. The one thing that the fairground workers don't want is the police hanging around or making inquiries around their stalls or rides. In consequence there was an immediate reply, "He's working tonight, but he's kipping in the big van overt-here (at the same time pointing to a large covered articulated trailer). I think you'll find he's there now".

We left the ride and our vehicle and walked over to the van that had been pointed out to us. The sides of the van were canvas covered and strapped, so we undid a few straps, moved the cover and got onto the back of the van without much difficulty. In the van there were sleeping bags, bits of belongings and, two people sleeping there, a male and a female, the male was definitely our wanted man, because his back was exposed and there was the `hunt tattoo`, what an identification aid.

On the two van dwellers realizing that there was someone present they both sat up and, we told them who we were and, I put to the male his name, which he admitted to and, then the formalities of arresting him were completed and he was told to get dressed, because he was leaving with us.

We then inquired as to the identity of the female and asked for proof of it. She said that she hadn't got any. We asked her age and where she was from, it was evident that she had virtually no belongings and, after having searched the the van it was clear that she traveled lightly. She gave us a name and, said that she was seventeen, she then told us that she was from Liverpool and, her only `back-up` to that claim was her Liverpudlian accent. She couldn't give us any address just saying that she was traveling with the fair. We asked which ride or stall she was working on and, she said, "The box office at the House of Horrors". I said, "We'll check on the way to the van". To which we replied, "There's no need to. I legged it from the approved school (It so happened that there was a girl's approved school in the area), a couple of nights ago". She was also told that she was traveling back with us.

At this time we had no requirement to question them further, because of the sound fingerprint evidence against our burglar, which we hadn't told him about so far, but having got the evidence we could put it to him once we were questioning him back at the station. With regard to the abscondor we had no requirement to question her further at this time because she had admitted being an abscondor from custody and, she was obviously at large after having received a custodial sentence.

We walked them back to our C.I.D. van, which wasn't the most comfortable of vehicles to travel in when deposited in the back, but at least the rear doors locked to prevent escape and, we were able to sit in the front, but even that was with the minimum of comfort. They were told that they were going back to our police area and, having travelled from there they obviously knew that they had a five or six mile journey to endure.

On our return to the divisional H.Q., we took them both into the charge room to book them in and, dealt with the female first with her being a juvenile. The Sergeant then sent for a policewoman, because of her being a female and under the age of eighteen to act as a Matron whilst she was in custody. She was asked the usual questions by the charge room Sergeant for the completion of the charge forms and, she gave her correct name and admitted to being an abscondee from the Approved School, to which the Sergeant said, "We'll get someone from there to come down to be with her when she's interviewed". At the same time he told one of the P.C's present to ring the establishment and get a member of staff from there to attend, for them to be present during the interview and to take her into their custody and escort her back to the Approved School. She was then taken by the policewoman to the juvenile detention room, which was another name for a police cell, to be interviewed on the arrival of the officer from the School.

We now had to deal with the burglar and, introduce him to the charge room Sergeant to have him deposited in the cell block for him to await being interviewed. I then told the Sergeant who the prisoner was and, that I had arrested him for a series of burglaries. It was just at that time that the Detective Inspector and the Detective

Sergeant walked into the charge room, for some other reason than seeing me and, obviously they had heard what I was saying about the arrest and the fingerprint evidence, which at that time the prisoner knew nothing about and neither did the boss or the Sergeant (that was their fault for not checking my mail or having it checked while I was on leave).

The Detective Inspector beckoned me into the corridor outside the charge-room and, I answered to his call. "What's all this?", he said. I explained to him that fingerprints had matched the burglar to the eight burglaries and, I had found out that he was working on the fairground in the next door forces' area, that I had tried to contact them but couldn't, so I had to act quickly. I also explained to him that I had tried to contact him before leaving our county to make the inquiries, but that I had been unable to find him and, having found out what a wanderer the burglar was , then it was absolutely necessary to go and find him if we could and, we were fortunate enough to locate him and arrest him, together with his girlfriend who we had also brought back as an absconder from the Approved School. I then said, "By the way Sir, I did think that you would have known about the fingerprint identifications, because nearly all the letters confirming the identifications were on your desk waiting for me to come back from leave, they'd been there for four or five days and they'd all been opened, so they did need acting on as quickly as possible". "Yes. Yes, of course it did, but whose the female that you've arrested?". I then told him of how she had been with the prisoner, but that she was a juvenile and, that all the correct procedure had been adhered to because she was an absconder from the Approved School and that we were awaiting a mentor from there to be with her when she was interviewed. "Well, she may have committed some offenses as well, so I'll leave it to you. Let me know what results you get". It was surprising that after I'd mentioned about there being no action on the correspondence when I was away, that there was no `piss taking about the doctor's wife` and, it was just a matter of `get on with it!`.

The officer from the Approved School arrived and, the young girl was brought from the `juvenile detention room` by the policewoman to the interview room. The girl obviously knew the officer from the Approved School and, the identity of the girl was confirmed immediately by the officer, who just said with a soft tone, "Welcome back. This officer and the policewoman have some questions to ask you and, it would be better if you just tell them if you have been responsible for anything while you've been away. Just get it all finished now if you have".

She was pensive and, then she said, "I want to get back and have a good bath, I've been living rough with him, it was only because we were from the same place that I went with him".

She was asked the inevitable question then, "Where did you meet him?". "On the last fairground that he was on", she said, "We seemed to get on straight away, we were from the same place and, we got pissed after he'd finished on the rides and, we just talked in the back of the truck that he was kipping in. He told me that he'd done some jobs around here and that he was doing another one for what he could get and that he was moving on then". She then went on, "Let's get it all finished, because I've only done one job with him". I then said, "Which one was that?". "It was a bungalow that we broke into, it was near here(meaning the police station-she obviously knew the area), we got in and she was in bed, but we went all through and just got some cash and a few ornaments to sell. That's all I've done since I've been out."

A statement was then taken from her and, she was then placed in the hands of the officer from the Approved School and in her custody to be seen at a later date, to be charged if it was thought appropriate so to do.

Now came the interview with our identified burglar, there was not much that he could deny, his prints were there, it was a rock solid identification that he was responsible for the eight burglaries that had been given to me to investigate, so in he came. I was in the interview room with Nigel and, I said, "You know us by now and who we are, but to be sure I'll introduce us again, which I did. I then said, "When you were being booked in in the charge room you heard me tell the Sergeant that you had been identified by fingerprint examination as being responsible for eight burglaries in this area. I'm now going to put to you the circumstances of the burglaries and ask for your comments." Obviously he was under caution, but he replied, "If you've got me dabs on all of them then I'm bang to rights, so yeh, it was me".

I then asked him, "Were you with anyone else when you did those jobs?". "No" was his immediate reply. "Are you sure", I said, "because your girlfriend has told us that she was with you when you went into a bungalow which was below the woods and you got some cash and a few other things. Is that right?".

"Well you know that I did it, yes she was with me, she's told you, but that's the only one I did with her.

I then went on, with Nigel's assistance, to place all the burglaries before him and, he admitted the lot, albeit that he didn't have much option by virtue of the evidence of the singularity of the fingerprint evidence.

The young lady was also again interviewed at her place of institution to give the necessary admission statement, which she did, but she was not at all happy at the time, because she had just been medically examined, only to be found that she was pregnant. She was eventually charged with the joint aggravated burglary of the doctor's house and was sentenced to a further six moths. It was likely that her child would have been born around then and it is hoped that the authorities looked after her and her new born.

The prisoner was charged singularly with seven burglaries and jointly with the female for the burglary at the doctor's house and, was to be held in custody until he appeared before the Magistrate's Court the following morning. He so appeared before the Magistrates and, after the circumstances had been put to the Bench, the Magistrates remanded him in custody to again appear before their Court to be committed to the Court of Quarter Sessions and, some weeks later he was so committed.

In the interim period all eight Complaints had to be seen and informed that unfortunately non of their possessions had been recovered, but that the burglaries had been detected and, that the person(s) who had been arrested were to appear before the Court in the near future when the case was listed and, that they would be informed of the date of the hearing.

Appointments were made to see all of the Complainants and, the first seven were seen and they were all extremely pleased with the outcome. I then had to visit the doctor's wife to explain to her the outcome of the investigations. I went to the door with some trepidation, but it was opened by "The Lady of the House", who was scantily dressed to say the least. She invited me in saying that it was nice to see me again. She went on to say, "Let's go onto the patio to talk, I've been out there sunbathing all morning and it's absolutely beautiful". We went through the dining room, through the patio doors onto the patio where there was a table and chairs, together with a couple of sun beds. On the table there was a bottle of wine and two glasses. "Let's have a glass of wine, you pour", she said as she sat on one of the sun beds. I sat on a chair at the table and said, "I'll pour you a glass, but I wont join you, thank you anyway". "I know your on duty and that I shouldn't encourage you to drink on duty, but one wont harm", she said. As I was pouring her a drink I said, "Thank you anyway, but I am in a bit of a rush, so I'll explain to you what happened and then get back to the station".

A brief resume was given to her and, I retreated as quickly as possible thinking that the sooner her husband returned it would be better for all.

The Quarter Sessions hearing date arrived and, the fairground burglar pleaded guilty to all the burglaries and, was sentenced to four years imprisonment.

The doctor's wife was present at Court with the doctor, thankfully. They had attended to see the outcome of the case and, he was a nice bloke!.

MARRIAGE AND A CHANGE OF DIRECTION

Twelve weeks soon passed and the wedding day loomed, in those twelve weeks after I'd finished the burglary inquiries, I'd been engaged on routine C.I.D. duties, assisting uniform officers with their criminal inquiries, putting court files together and sorting out a couple of domestic assaults.

The time seemed to fly past, because of the work commitments and, with moving into the flat that I was renting from the week prior to the marriage I had quite a bit of work to do decorating, cleaning and furnishing, but there was quite a bit of appreciated help from colleagues and friends and that made the task that much easier.

My intended at that time had not seen the flat, but I had described it to her and explained what I was doing during the numerous telephone calls that had been made, she had not been over in the interim because of the geographical problems, but the flat itself was very presentable and, the views were spectacular.

In the interim my future wife had handed in her notice at the school she was teaching at and, at the same time had been applying for teaching posts in North Wales. I had been getting the local and regional papers to see that there were many vacancies for primary school teachers in the area and, I also knew that it was the positive position of the Education Authority that the policy was to employ fifty per cent Welsh speaking teachers and fifty per cent non-Welsh speaking teachers and, that was stated in every teaching vacancy advertised The truth was , that at an interview the question was asked whether or not the interviewee spoke welsh and, if the answer was `No`, then the candidate would not be considered for the advertised post, despite having completed a Teacher's Training Course in Wales. It was discrimination at its best, because she was always being turned away for not being conversant in the Welsh language, mitigating factors, such as , husband's ability to converse in the Welsh language, moving to Wales after marriage and, having been educated in Wales, didn't count.

The date of the marriage arrived and, a flood of relatives and friends descended at the arranged East Coast venue and, `the Welsh contingent` , after their long drive, were all happy and content with the arrangements for their comfort for the nights prior to and after the marriage date. All went well on the appointed date and, the ceremony being over, the bride and groom departed for some relaxation at a resort on the east coast. It so happened that the weather was appalling, albeit that it was Autumn, so it was decided to cut short the honeymoon and, head back westward with essential belongings and wedding presents and, that's what we did. It also enabled the bride to see the marital flat earlier, plus it would give some extra time to settle in, prior to me going back to work.

We collected our belongings from the `in-laws-home` and, whatever wedding presents we could squeeze into the car and, then set off on the then six or seven hour journey to our destination and, new home in North Wales. We arrived tired and worn out, but on our arrival outside the flat the view from the front was one of the sun setting over the bay and, that was totally magnificent in a cloud cleared sky. It was super and, I couldn't help saying, "Wait until you've seen the view of the mountains at the back tomorrow, it's really something, but let's get the cases in first to avoid having to do it in the morning", which we did.

The car was emptied and the contents were piled into the spare bedroom to be cleared later. In the meantime the kettle had been put on and boiled and, having brewed we sat in the front living room just taking in the view of the bay in the moonlight.

The following morning duly arrived and , on opening the bedroom curtains, that gave a view to the rear, that exposed the most magnificent view of the mountains, so if you looked to the front there was the sea and the bay and to the rear the mountains. The flat itself was also extremely nice and, my decorating and furnishings were appreciated.

I had seven days left of my leave and, because there was no offer of a teaching post so far, inquiries were made at the Education Department together with more applications for teaching vacancies as advertised in the local and regional newspapers. One advertisement was for a teaching post in a private school near to the police headquarters, but it was only part time, the advertisement was answered successfully and it resulted in a successful appointment. She enjoyed the teaching , but a permanent local Education Authority post was wanted together with a desire to teach in primary education on a full time basis, but all advertisements continued to be advertised as `Welsh Essential`, despite that the applications were submitted and declined because there was no ability to converse in the Welsh language by the applicant, albeit that there was a declaration by her of an intent to improve and learn on the present meager ability to so converse .

I returned to work and, my wife continued to work part time at the private school, with the frustration of knowing that she was more than qualified for the Local Education posts that were advertised, she even went to Welsh language lessons, but even that made no difference to cracking the `Welsh Essential" label.

The flat was super, my job was super and enjoyable and' gave me a great deal of satisfaction, but my wife's predicament by virtue of her being unable to speak welsh and, not being able to gain a suitable permanent position, caused a great deal of frustration to us both. We both wanted to progress in our respective careers and, I was, but she wasn't, because of the believed narrow mindedness of the Local Authority and their Education Department, who were totally going against their stated employment policy with regard to teaching qualifications.

However life went on as the frustration was growing, but it became such that I decided to air my opinion of the County Education Authority with regard to their prejudiced view on the recruiting of teachers and of the police service with regard to their similar attitude, both advertising that recruitment would be on a fifty per cent Welsh speaking and a fifty per cent non Welsh speaking intake, but that if the truth was known there was a total bar against non-Welsh speaking applicants. My view was therefore aired by writing to the local press and the North Wales press, with the letters bearing my signature, which did not declare whether it was Mr. or Mrs. who was the author of the letters. The contents of the letters obviously hit the Councilors where it was meant to hurt, because there were immediate complaints from local and County Councilors regarding the content of the letters, to the Chief Constable about me entering into a political scene. At that time, police officers were subjected to disciplinary proceedings if it was found that they had become politically involved in any issue(s) which were of a political nature.

The complaints had to be investigated and, I was duly summonsed into the Divisional Superintendent's office to tell me that the Chief Constable wanted to see me the following Monday at the force headquarters so that the matter could be investigated with me being able to put my side of the story before matters were taken further. Oh hell!, that was going to be another one and a half hours drive in the divisional van to the force headquarters. I didn't know which was going to be worse the driving or the interview.

There was a week to go, so it was a matter of getting on with the job, albeit that the forthcoming appearance before the Chief was foremost in my mind.

Just after having been in the Superintendent's office I was summonsed to the Detective Inspector's office. I ventured towards the door with some trepidation, wondering what the hell next could go wrong, I knocked on the door and, was invited in by the usual unwelcoming voice. "Now then", he said, "I understand that you're now trying to enter the world of political journalism, but there's work to be done here before you progress along that path". He was obviously inviting a reply, so I chose not to answer. He continued, "There's a girl in the reception who's complaining about being badly assaulted, her story doesn't add up, so go and see her and get rid of her, from what's been said to me she's a total time waster".

My duty on this day had so far been one of being castigated by senior officers who ultimately didn't want to be associated with my opinions and views with regard to the running of the Education Authority and, they certainly didn't want associating with the argument that was being put forward concerning the single minded attitude of the Authorities that there was a necessity to be able to converse in the Welsh language to even apply for a job in the area.

Nevertheless, there was work to be done and the young lady in the reception had to be seen regarding her "dubious" report of being badly sexually assaulted.

Upon getting to the reception the constable who had been dealing with the report came up to me and said, "This girls been telling me a story that's so far fetched for the last hour and a half that I don't know whether or not to believe her".

"What's she been telling you?", I asked. "Well", he said, "She lives in a flat in the town on her own and, she's been there for about three months. She moved from her home town about forty miles away after being transferred within the structure of her firm on being promoted in the admin' department. She says that she had fallen in love with a man who worked for the same firm who had been transferred down here in a managerial position and, he is now living with his wife in a village nearby".

As the Constable was telling me the story I was at the same time reading his notes which told me that the young lady was nineteen years of age, extremely pretty , small in stature and well spoken and presented and, showing no emotion. The boy friend was twenty five years of age, living in his own house with his wife and, there were no children. Apparently the boyfriend's wife knew nothing about the clandestine relationship, but the complainant was hoping that her man friend would leave his wife and live with her. When she got the transfer after his move, he had found the flat for her and, helped her move into the accommodation. He had been repeatedly telling her that he was going to leave his wife and move in with her, but that move had not, at that time, happened.

The flat where she lived was the whole of the ground floor of an end terraced house. It was completely self-contained and, access could be gained by the front door which lead into the flat from the street and, by walking down a ten-foot at the side of the house, into a yard and by then going through a rear door directly into the flat. When entry had been gained through the rear door, which was of full frosted glass with wooden surround it gave entry to the kitchen which was well equipped and extremely tidy. If, on entry, you turned right, you would cross the kitchen and come to the bathroom. If, on entering, you turned to the left you would enter the living room where on the wall opposite was the fireplace and diagonally across was another door into the bedroom. In the living room was a three piece suite, with a chair as you entered, a settee beyond that chair and, another chair near to the bedroom door. The officer had then recorded that the flat was extremely neat and tidy. I felt as if I'd already visited the accommodation.

The officer then said, "She tells me that she left work, that day, about five o'clock and walked home, arriving there about ten minutes later. She says that she opened the rear gate and went through the back yard and opened the rear door with her key. When she got into the house, she put her handbag in the kitchen as usual and, then went into the bedroom, undressed and put her dressing gown on. She was expecting her boyfriend to call at anytime, so it was her intention to get a bath and get dressed ready to go out with him when he arrived. She'd got her clean clothes out of the dressing table drawer in her bedroom and took them into the living room where she placed her pants, suspender belt and stockings on the settee with her dress. Having done this she said that she went through the kitchen to the bathroom taking with her, her bra'. After she had a bath she said that she put her bra' on and her dressing gown and walked into the living room. She then said that she was about to go into the bedroom to do her hair when she heard a knock on the back door and, thinking that it was her boyfriend arriving early, she immediately went to the door and opened it."

I then said, being impatient, "What happened then?". The constable then continued, "When she opened the back door, she saw a man, not large in stature, but wearing a dark mackintosh and a red hood which completely covered his head. The hood she said had two slits in it for the eyes which she could not see clearly and a slit for the mouth. She said he had a gun with him and he waved it at her and told her to move back into the flat. She said that she couldn't recall what her feelings were, but she just backed away".

I said, "What sort of state was she in when she was telling you all this?". "She was just normal, she didn't seem to be upset at all", he said, and then went on, "I asked her what her feelings were and she just said that she backed away and he followed her and closed the door behind him. She said that she walked backwards into the living room and sat on the arm of the first chair in the living room, as the intruder had a quick look around the kitchen and followed her into the living room".

I then asked him if she was squealing and shouting for help at this time and, what was the intruder saying to her if anything. The officer went on, "I've asked her that and, she said that she daren't say anything or shout for help. She said he walked up to her and pushed her off the arm of the chair onto the floor. She said that she was frightened and petrified and that she fell with her head near to the fireplace and her feet towards the kitchen door. At this time she said the man was still brandishing his gun and, she was too frightened to move or do anything. She said the intruder then put the gun on the chair and then knelt down at the side of her and released her dressing gown belt and pulled her dressing gown open and started to fondle her breasts".

I interrupted the officer and asked, "Was she making any attempt to struggle or get away from him?" and, he said that he had asked her that question, but she'd told him that she was so frightened that she couldn't move.

"Was she upset when she was telling you, or was she embarrassed or upset in anyway?", I further questioned, and the P.C. said, "No, not at all. She was really calm and didn't show any signs of being upset and she went on to tell me her story without any prompting or interruption and said that he picked the black stockings off the settee and tied them around her ankles and, he then sat astride her waist and reached out for a scarf that was on the chair and tied it around her mouth. After having bound and gagged her the assailant remained sitting across her waist, placed his hands behind him and pulled her legs up and opened her knees and placed his fingers inside her vagina. He then leaned forward and took a candle from out of a wine bottle that was on the hearth and, up to this time the assailant had not done anything to himself to rouse himself".

"She then said that he put the candle into her vagina and moved it about to simulate copulation and with his other hand continued to fondle her breasts", said the officer and, he continued, "She said that he didn't remove his hood or any other clothing while he continued to assault her, from what she said was for ages. Then suddenly she said he got up from sitting on her, picked up the gun from the chair and then immediately left the flat by the way he had entered without saying a word. She then told me that she lay there for some time, being too afraid to move, but eventually she removed the scarf and the stockings and the candle and remained sitting on the floor with her head on her arm, crying".

I couldn't avoid asking the question, "Do you believe her?", to which the officer replied, "I don't know. She went on to tell me that her boyfriend arrived shortly after and he found her crying and she told him what had happened and, he immediately wanted to telephone the police, but she wouldn't let him. She said that her boyfriend comforted her and she went and had another bath and, dressed in different clothes and they both went out traveling in the boyfriend's car, to a nearby village pub for a drink. The boyfriend was all the while trying to get her to report it, but she still said that she didn't want the police involved. When they left the pub, the boyfriend without her permission and against her will, drove straight to the police station and made her get out of the car and report it".

By this time I was asking myself whether the story was too well rehearsed, was she trying to get her boyfriend to go and live with her permanently and show his true feelings towards her? I was bothered also by the way she had said that she had answered the door and, then had not screamed or tried to fight off the assailant. I was also questioning why she was so cool, calm and collected and, not showing any other emotions? The only emotions she had shown was to her boyfriend when she told him, so was that a further sign of trying to get him to leave his wife?

Having had the story told to me by the initial police officer who interviewed her in a very detailed fashion, it was my turn to see her. If what she was saying to us was true then she wanted all the help, compassion and security that she could be shown, so I went into the interview room where she had been placed to find her with a policewoman partaking of a cup of tea and talking with the policewoman absolutely normally - not in a way that you would expect a female to be after having been allegedly so seriously assaulted.

She'd been interviewed by the P.C. who was able to tell me in detail her story, she had also been in the presence of the policewoman for some time and her story continued to be the same to her and, I then found that the Detective Inspector had also been to see her and, having heard the story he had left the scene of the Inquiry only to pass it on to me, because basically he didn't believe her, so there wasn't going to be any detection in his estimation. When he passed the inquiry to me he certainly didn't tell me that he had seen the complainant. I had had my differences with the Detective Inspector now on two occasions previously, so I was determined to get to the bottom of what had happened.

The D.I. had remonstrated with me for engaging the press on a previous inquiry and, he had shown no support for me on the so called political issue of my wife gaining employment within a Welsh essential situation within the educational field and, once again he was fielding out to me a criminal investigation where he thought there was going to be no end result.

I introduced myself to the young lady and, normally when interviewing females who were reporting being indecently assaulted or raped, one had to show understanding and, comfort them and speak to them at the same time in an endearing manner, but with this young lady she was positive, showing no emotion and, she was certainly putting herself over as being a very strong character.. Nevertheless I reassured her that it was necessary to go over her story again and, that that was our job and that all we wanted was a successful conclusion to the inquiry. She said, "I don't know how many more times I'll have to tell you. I don't think that you believe me, but you can do what you want. I didn't want to come here in the first place".

I went through her story with her in great detail and inquired of her as to why she appeared to be so nonchalant, to which she replied, "What do I have to do, do I have to cry all the while I'm talking to you?". Her story remained the same as I had been told by the P.C., she was just resolute in everything that she said. I than asked her if she would undergo a medical examination by the police surgeon (who I had already placed on notice that I may require his services) and, she immediately said that she had no objection and indicated that she just wanted to get out of the station as quickly as possible. The Constable had taken a preliminary statement from her and, therefore for her sake it was essential that the medical examination was conducted as quickly as possible so that she could leave with her boyfriend on the basis that we could see her again to elaborate on the details of the assault within a more complex statement.

Within a very short period of time the Police Surgeon attended and, on examining her he found that there were no marks on her face, ankles or neck or indeed any other part of her body. On examining her internally he found a minute scratch on the wall of her vagina, but this he said, could have been caused at any time during intercourse or heavy petting and, she had stated that she was having regular sex with her boyfriend. There was therefor nothing conclusive from the medical examination.

Following the examination I went with the young lady and her boyfriend to her flat and, on seeing the layout, I left, telling them again that we would do everything we could to come to a successful conclusion.

I had prior to that seen the boyfriend on his own and, he had verified the details of the story that concerned him, but he too did not know whether or not to believe what his girlfriend had said. He was also well aware that she wanted him the leave his wife and go and live with her and, he admitted that he had on a number of occasions told her that that was his intention. He also admitted to me that in fact he had no intention of leaving his wife or their home and, he was sure that she was aware of that and she had he said become extremely emotional about it in the past.

All the immediate house to house inquiries revealed nothing, the indecency merchants who were known to reside in the area were seen and, all those and all other inquiries proved to be negative. Those inquiries were completed within a matter of days, so as the D.I. said the case could be written off.

It so happened that four days later there was a report from the adjoining sub-division that there had been an extremely serious assault in their area, the circumstances being that a female householder had been in her garden when a man wearing a red hood and a dark mackintosh had tried to force her into the house and that at the same time he had pointed a gun at her. Bravely, this lady who was in her forties said that she had hit the intruder with her peg bag causing the pegs to scatter when the bag broke and, the assailant, having been hit, ran off clearing the garden fence in one and disappeared.

On receipt of the complaint all available officers had been detailed to search the area together with two dog handlers and their dogs and, within some ten to fifteen minutes a call had been received by the sub-divisional headquarters from one of the officers to say that he had just arrested an eighteen year old male who was wearing a dark mackintosh. The officer then had said that after having questioned the man he had asked him to empty his pockets, which he reluctantly did, only to reveal a red coloured hood and, on doing so he had attempted to run off, hence the arrest of the eighteen year old on suspicion of being the person responsible for the assault on the complainant.

I went to the sub-divisional headquarters where the man was being held, the journey took about twenty minutes and spoke to the arresting Constable, who said that as he was approaching the suspect he saw him throwing something over a hedge, but he hadn't been able to check or search the area because of having to hold onto the suspect.

The arrested male had been placed in the only cell at the police station and, he had not been questioned further than those questions asked of him at the time of his arrest. The officer and I then went to the place of arrest and we searched the area where he said he had seen the suspect throwing something over a hedge and, our search of the area was rewarded with the find of a gun. It was a replica, it was metal and so real that it could have fooled an expert firearms officer at first sight. After having returned to the divisional headquarters with the weapon, we found that the prisoner had also been transferred there from the sub-divisional headquarter and, a firearms officer examined the gun and, had to take it apart to be sure that it had not been modified to have been turned into a firearm. The examination revealed that it hadn't, but that was how real looking it was.

Interview time had arrived and, I went to see the prisoner with the Constable that had arrested him. We introduced ourselves. We had with us his mackintosh, his hood and, the firearm. We put it to him that they were his and that he had been wearing the hood and mackintosh when he assaulted the lady that hit him with the clothes peg bag, straight away there was an admission. We then showed him the gun and, asked the inevitable question as to whether or not it was his, to which he replied, "Yes, but it isn't a real one. It wouldn't have hurt her". I said, "Well why did you have it with you?". "I just wanted to frighten her", he replied. "Why did you try to force that lady into her home?". "Well it gets me going and I just wanted sex with her", he replied.

"So you agree that today you assaulted the lady in the garden and tried to force her into her home to have sex with her?". "Yes", he replied. "You understand that what you have admitted to is an extremely serious offense, do you?", I asked and, received the reply, as a simple, "Yes".

I then said to him, "Well, I have a much more serious matter to put to you, there was an assault on a young lady in her home about a week ago not far from here, when someone knocked on the back door and , she was forced into her flat and seriously indecently assaulted and subjected to a humiliating experience by someone wearing a red hood and a dark mackintosh. It can't be anyone else but you, can it?". To which he replied a bland, "No".

I was delighted that my reported crime had been solved and so had the sub-divisional crime.

It was now time to get the admission on paper in the form of a statement under caution, which was taken in great detail about both incidents. He was also questioned as to whether or not he had committed other offenses, but he was positive in saying that he hadn't and, there were no more offenses of a similar nature reported so he had to be believed that, in his words, he was, "just starting out". Undoubtedly he meant that he was starting out on a road of serious sexual attacks on females and, it was to be hoped that his early arrest would prevent other such attacks. The prisoner's admissions were such that the statements of both complainants were absolutely verified and, he was duly charged and kept in the police cells until his court appearance the following morning when he was remanded in custody until a committal date.

My first thought was to get in touch with the first lady who had been assaulted and tell her about the arrest, the arresting officer was going to tell the second lady who had been subjected to the assault of the outcome. I went around to the complainant's flat, only to find that she had moved. Further inquiries revealed that she had had a massive `bust up` with her boy friend after his wife had found out about their affair and, she had returned to her home town to live with her parents.

I, myself, felt particularly badly about having doubted her story, although I was sure in my own mind that I had done everything I could and given her every consideration possible. I had her parent's telephone number on the file, so I was able to contact her and tell her of the arrest, needless to say there was a great relief on her part, albeit that she expressed the relief in the terms that it would never have happened if she hadn't fallen in love with a married man and followed him foolishly.

Needless to say, the Detective Inspector had been told of the arrest and, he had also been told of the outcome of the interview, which I confirmed to him when I saw him. Sadly, he was himself, more concerned about his crime statistics than the wellbeing of the injured parties saying, "Well, it won't do our figures any harm, will it?". I couldn't resist a reply saying, "Well you were going to write it off, but of course if you'd have done so the percentage detection figures would have been the same wouldn't they, Sir!".

There was a plea of guilty by the accused and when he appeared before the Quarter Sessions he was sentenced to four years imprisonment, which to a certain degree consoled the injured ladies, but I'm sure it didn't obliterate the awful experiences from their minds.

I'm certain that the first victim must have been in a state of total shock to be able to give the story in the way that she did, because I am certain that no one who had experienced what she obviously had, could be so matter of fact about the circumstances as she was, if indeed she was not traumatized

I suppose the moral to the story is, the more unbelievable a story is, the more likely it is to be true.

My interview with the Chief was two days after the arrest and, I traveled to the Headquarters in the divisional van, the journey was exactly what I had expected, it was a total pain to have to travel in such a dilapidated vehicle that shouldn't have been on the road, never mind being a police vehicle.

I arrived at the H.Q. offices in good time and presented myself for the interview. I was duly summonsed to the Chief's office only to be asked by him, as he referred to the newspapers in front of him which had publicized the offending letters, "Well, what's all this about? What are you doing entering into the political field? You must be well aware that as a police officer it is a disciplinary offense to engage in the political scene or make political statements and, your letters have placed you in that category". I replied, "Those letters to the papers are signed and, my name appears after them, but they have omitted to put (Mrs.) after the name, we are after all married and she has my name and I can't account for the journalistic omission of not including the title of the writer". I had revirsed that reply during the whole of the journey in that decrepit van that I had traveled in to the interview, which made the journey even worse.

The reply from the Chief was shear relief to my ears, he said, "So, there isn't much I can do about it is there. You're wife obviously has a mind of her own and, the letters are extremely well written and express an opinion. There is not a lot more to be said about that then, so I will reply to the complaints in the appropriate manner". His tone of voice immediately then changed and he continued, "You will be training on Thursday, won't you?. We've got a couple of hard matches ahead, so I expect to see you there training hard, you look to be in good condition".

There was a man who had remembered my recruitment and, seen me on the rugby and football fields on a number of occasions and, immediately adopted a sensible and positive attitude to the complaints of "My entering into the political field". At that time it was also a disciplinary offense if a spouse of an officer made political statements, but the common sense of the Chief saw the stupidity of that and, took no notice of it, hence him casting it aside.

However, on the way back to my divisional headquarters, I decided that I had to move on to give my wife a chance to follow her teaching career where she could pursue her ambition and, I could follow mine, in what would be a totally different area and environment. I then decided that I was going to apply for a transfer to a City force on the east coast of England, knowing full well that at that time transfers were few and far between and frowned upon and that the probationary period would be extended by a period of nine months for the new force to make their own mind up about my ability.

My wife would be near her family and friends and, she had already applied for teaching positions within the area resulting in offers of teaching placements. I then placed my application for transfer, which was looked at in the most dismayed manner by my force, but it resulted in me being given an interview date at the Headquarters of the force I had applied to, I attended the interview, which was totally different to what I had previously experienced, to be appointed an officer in a force that was four times as big as the one I was serving in, in a City area where every aspect of policing was different. Two interviews over and, I was accepted, which meant that my probationary period would be extended by nine months and that I would be back in uniform. I accepted the position despite those senior officers in my home force saying that I was doing the wrong thing and, `that a rolling stone gathered no moss`, giving me the inference that all, I had done so far would be forgotten.

It mattered not what was said, I couldn't leave my wife to not be able to progress her career because of the narrowness of the mind of the Welsh education authority, so it was departure from the scene of North Wales to a City of considerable size on the mid east coast of England that was renowned for its fishing heritage and, where we both could enhance our careers.

THE DEPARTURE FROM ONE FORCE TO ANOTHER

On the acceptance of the transfer by both forces, the accepting force accepted a date of transfer and, then gave a period of four days for the first duty appearance by the transferee, once again to be fitted out with uniform and to be initiated into the force procedure.

It was at this time that the uniform was in the process of changing, from the dog collar to the `V` neck. I was issued within those four days with `V` neck tunics and separate collar shirts. So what, that was the dress and, it had to be adhered to and, the Chinese laundries made a bomb out of it by starching the collars. The regime was such that short sleeves were not worn at any time and, head dress was worn at all times, whether you were within or without a vehicle. Smartness was the call of the day. Yes, it was back to uniform duties and, the way of working was completely different. I had been due to finish my two years probation, but with having transferred an extra nine months was added for my new force to get to assess my ability. That mattered not because my wife was appointed to a teaching position on her first application, so we could now both progress our careers and get on with our lives.

The first day of duty was the usual initiation of being shown around the divisional headquarters and, the division that I had been posted to was the City Center, so not only was there the divisional headquarters, but also the force headquarters within the same building. The establishment was four times greater than my first force and, the atmosphere was impersonal, by that I mean that the majority of constables just wanted to sign on duty, do their eight hours and sign off, They appeared to have no interest in any job that they were sent to, other than putting in an appearance at the scene of a reported incident, accident (road traffic or general) or crime. After a very short period of time I realized the reason, which was because once they had attended at a scene the inquiry was then taken over by a specialist department and, they had no further involvement. By far the majority of the constables were of ten to thirty years experience and had become somewhat stayed in their ways.

The first week of my duties was then spent in the traffic department to be shown the City itself by attending incidents reported in various parts of the City. The vehicles had just had wirelesses fitted in them, but the officers on foot or in C.I.D. were not equipped with personal radios and still relied on the system of calling the control at agreed times.

The following two weeks were arranged to be a week of a days shift and then a week of nights shift to be accompanied by an experienced P.C. of some years service to get to know the City Center and the immediate industrial areas which were surrounded by streets with small two up and two down terraced houses leading off them.

It was during these two weeks that I realized the lack of interest that the older constables showed in doing the job, there was a total "couldn't care less" attitude. The night shift was a complete nonsense, because the copper who was showing me around was only interested in looking through chinks in curtains where there were lights on to see what was going on inside. He was creeping down terraces and into back yards of the two up and two down properties wherever he saw a light on to peer through any curtain that he could find remotely open to see if he could see and witness any sexual activity inside. He even one night went to the lengths of climbing up a lamp post and onto a wall to look into a bedroom window. I had never come across this sort of Police behavior previously and, couldn't bring myself to condone it, but it was happening and I didn't need to be part of it.

I was amazed to hear certain officers prior to the pre-duty parade explaining graphically what they had seen as a result of their creeping around terraced houses and peering through the chinks in the curtains. They would even arrange to meet up with officers on adjoining beats to show them the spectacle of the love nests that they had found. There was not a lot I could do about it, except to think, "How sad".

The day shift was one of being engulfed by people working and shopping in the city center and, doing point duty at extremely busy junctions. The point duty was for a period of four hours, standing in a box controlling the vehicles and the public and then having a break and, completing the rest of the duty waving your arms about. After a full shift on point duty there was no requirement to go training or to the gym, because the upper half of the torso had been exercised to the full.

It was a totally different scene to what I had been used to and, I didn't particularly like it, but I had made my bed so to speak and just had to get on with it.

I was now, after two weeks initiation, on my own and, it so happened that my first week was a week of night duties. All properties on the beat had to be checked both back and front twice a night and all points had to be met, that being that the duty sergeant would stipulate a point , whether it be a police box or a geographical point, where he could visit you or call you.

After about five nights I was out on my beat which included an arterial road into the city, very near to the center, I was on the outskirts of the beat when I saw the officer on the adjoining beat carrying a dustbin onto my beat and starting to take it down a passage way which was behind the shops which nearly all had flats above. The officer was portly in stature and had about twenty plus years experience in the force and displayed a fine line of medal ribbons above the left breast pocket of his uniform. I straight away asked him what he was doing only to be told that he was going behind the Chinese laundry where two of the daughters flaunted themselves in their altogether after getting a bath and, he wanted the dustbin to see over the wall. I couldn't believe my ears and , immediately told him that he could "bugger off back to his own beat", that didn't go down very well and, it certainly didn't stop him going to the rear of the Chinese laundry.

I followed him to where he placed the bin behind the Chinese laundry to enable him to look over the wall to view the scene of the naked daughters. I literally couldn't believe what I was seeing and, certainly wasn't going to condone it on my beat, so I straight away told him that I was making an entry in my note book of what had happened and, I also told him that if I was questioned about the entry then I would state what had happened. At the same time I reminded him of what the situation would be if someone had spotted his activity wearing a helmet doing what he was doing and, that the first person to be spoken to would be me, simply because it was my beat. He wasn't too happy at what I was saying and there were a few explicits expressed about my Welsh background, needless to say there was not much rapport between us thereafter.

Three weeks later matters didn't improve, I was again on night duty and beginning to think that I had joined a force full of perverts. I was on a totally different beat when I attended at a point at a police pillar amongst terraced houses very near the city center. There was no blue light flashing on the pillar, so that was the indication that I wasn't wanted to attend at any incident. It was about one o'clock in the morning and, further down the street where the pillar was situated, was a C.I.D. car parked at the end of a terrace. Something must be going on, I thought, but why haven't I been contacted when I attended at the point?.

The terrace the C.I.D. car was parked at the end of was a terrace of six houses with out houses with flat roofs to the rear. I went into the terrace and all was well to the front, so I went around the back, only to find two C.I.D. officers and four uniform officers on one of the flat roofs of an outhouse peering into the house, obviously watching something to their interest. It couldn't have been any criminal activity that they were watching , because it being my beat I would have known about it. It was obvious that they were watching , in their depraved way, some sort of sexual activity from their position on the flat roof, taking place in the living room. My thoughts were, "How sad could they be?" and "Who would get the blame for it if they were seen and a helmet was spotted?".

On seeing them I knew immediately what they were doing. They hadn't seen me, so I decided to state my position once and for all. I picked up two bin lids and crept towards the outhouse where they were all perched, and threw them against the wall, making one hell of a noise in the dead of night. Bodies scattered, the C.I.D. officers and the uniform officers were going in all directions, so were the helmets, lights were being switched on, and eventually doors were being opened.

I remained in the terrace and was able to settle the householders by telling them, on their inquiry, that I had heard the bang and arrived to investigate and, come to the conclusion that it must have been cats or an urban fox and, all was well.

Needless to say I was not the most popular person in the station later, but that mattered not, it served the purpose and I never saw them all there again.

It appeared that they were all watching a female R.A.F. officer who lived there with her parents, it seemed that she worked at an airbase on the outskirts of the city and, when she returned home late after her late shift, she would meet her boyfriend at her home and they would show their affections towards each other and, without their knowledge have it witnessed by perverted police officers.

I was beginning to hate and detest the move that I had made, but I was determined to carry on and make a success of it by going forward and getting on with my own career building.

THE MUFFLED BANG

Yet another week of nights, they seemed to come around all too often. The beat I was on had boundaries of tidal rivers to both the east and the south and, arterial roads leading in and out of the City to the north and west, encompassed within the boundaries were riverside warehouses and the dock side offices of the merchant traders. Dependant upon the tide times there was always the shipping activities on the rivers, the sound of their engines and movement and, the sound of their horns when the weather was inclement, which was regular. Also ingrained within the beat boundaries were the houses of those who serviced the industries, with the main streets and the numerous terraces off, together with the hostelries that serviced those that lived and worked in the area.

It was about two in the morning when I was walking along the dingiest of street between the housing and industrial areas, the street lighting was poor, the factories and industrial premises were making the usual noises and, the river traffic's noise was indeed peculiar to itself. There was then a contained explosion, something had seemed to explode in a controlled way. I was asking myself if it was something that happened every so often that I hadn't heard before but would get used to in the future or was it something in a factory that had exploded. The noise seemed to come from the adjoining street, so I cut through the maze of back entries and back passage ways to the next street to avoid having to go all the way around to the bottom of the street that I was on and turning to the next street. I found my way, believing that my navigation of the passageways and entries had benefited my arrival time at the scene of the "muffled bang".

On first arriving in the adjoining street there was nothing that could be seen, it was a dark night and the street lighting was poor to say the least, half of the street was industry and the other half terrace houses. No-one seemed to have been bothered by the "muffled noise", because no-one was about having been disturbed by the bang, so I was leaning further to the belief that it was an occasional noise that I could expect to hear in the future. I started looking around the occupied area and, nothing seemed untoward, but on looking back to the industrial end of the street I saw a dimly lit vehicle drive into the street and stop and the lights being switched off.

I made my way to where the vehicle had stopped and, as I neared I could see that there was some activity, exactly what I couldn't distinguish. The nearer I got I could see that the property the vehicle was outside was a post office with the door wide open. I didn't even know that there was a post office on this beat. The officer who had shown me around had obviously forgotten to tell me or show me, because he had obviously been too busy searching for chinks in curtains to study the sexual habits of those who resided in the area.

Anyway, I now knew that there was a post office and, from the smoke and the smell, it was plainly clear that the "muffled bang" was the safe being blown, that being an obvious bet which got the adrenalin flowing. I could see that there was quite a lot of activity inside and stuff being put into the car. My guess was that there were three of them, but I wasn't certain.

I got to the driver's side door of the car without any of them seeing me and saw that the window was open and. the car keys were in the ignition I was determined to take one of them, so I made my presence known to the first one that came out by "cracking" him with my torch. Fortunately he went down, there was no time to ask questions or caution him, he was mine with the cuffs on, which wasn't an easy job. There was the obvious noise made by the scuffle and, I could hear the shouts of the other two "Ger out it's the cops" as they heard the scramble that was going on near to the car.

I then saw one of the other two legging it down the road and, the other one showed himself at the door in somewhat of a mess, with quite a bit of injury to his face or so it appeared because of the blood that was on his face and, he was also limping badly. He didn't attempt to escape.

I had one with a bad head and cuffed and a second one with unknown injuries, but it was obvious that he couldn't move too far. I had no radio and, no houses in the immediate vicinity and, no-one had appeared to inquire about the additional noise that had occurred.

Both of them wanted hospital treatment, but that was the least of my worries, the question I was asking myself was "How the hell am I going to get them to the station?". I dragged the cuffed one into the building and, the other one just followed, moaning, I could only assume that his injuries had been caused by the explosion. The telephone was there to use, it was quite a relief to see it, until I tried it and found that the telephone line had obviously been damaged by the blast. I could now see, albeit that no lights would work, that the safe had been blown and two doors had been jemmied, including the front door.

I was stuck with two burglars/safe blowers and no communications to get help, the adrenalin was still burning and, the only solution to the problem was to use their car to get them to the station. I struggled with the two of them to the car and considered putting both of them in the boot, but decided against it and, managed to get them both in the back seats, which didn't make me feel too comfortable if I was going to drive.

I was convinced that neither of them was going very far, so I got into the driving seat, started the engine and drove off. It was only about a one and a half mile journey to the station, if that, but it seemed an eternity. I was also concerned that I had now left the post office open to all and sundry, but that couldn't be avoided. I drove the shortest way I knew to the station, but the car packed up about a hundred yards from the station and, there was no-way that it would re-start. There was therefore no alternative, but to walk the rest of the way, which we did after having locked the car with the Post Office takings in it.

Walking into the police station was one of the most comfortable feelings I have ever had. The officer on the reception opened the Charge Office door for me to walk into, only to be greeted by the Sergeant saying, "What the bloody hell have you got here?". I told him the story, only to have him say, "You should have taken them to the bloody hospital not brought them here!", and at the same time he was telling the charge room constable to call an ambulance and get a couple of officers to go with them. I then told him that I'd had no option but to leave the post office unattended and , that the car was locked but unattended with stolen property in it, to which he retorted, "The last bloody thing you should do is leave a scene unattended or stolen property not looked after, what the hell were you thinking about?!".

This was obviously a Sergeant who wanted an easy night and, any interference with his peace and tranquility caused an upset - just think of the paper work involved - he might not get off duty on time - yes, I'd again come upon another one that was totally not interested and idle to say the least.

The prisoners were booked in, the ambulance arrived and, under escort they went off to hospital, officers were sent to secure the scene of the break in and to recover the car. At this time the prisoners had not been questioned, so we had no idea who the third villain was.

I went back to the scene with the C.I.D. officers who had been called in and, as expected the safe had been blown, there was quite a bit of blood splattered about which had obviously come from the walking wounded prisoner and, there was a blooded scene near to where the car had been parked, obviously from the prisoner that I had had occasion to crack (the one that wasn't going to get away).

The car was recovered and, unbelievably it had stopped because of lack of petrol. In the car was cash, saving certificates, bank notes and, basically anything else they could throw in the boot, to sort out later.

Some two or three hours later the two patched up prisoners returned from the hospital, the one I had crusted had a few stitches, and had been x-rayed, and was fit to be interviewed, the second prisoner had self inflicted injuries from the blast, basically he had not retreated quickly enough, but he to was fit to be interviewed. The third one was still at large.

The interviews were about to start and, I was told to disappear and prepare a statement while the C.I.D. conducted the interviews. I couldn't believe what I was being told to do, basically to have no other part in the investigation except to submit a statement. There was no-way that I was going to accept that and, I insisted on being part of the interviewing scene, only to be told that that was the system, that the C.I.D. now took over. It was akin to world war three on my argument that they were my prisoners and that I was seeing the investigation through to its end and, eventually my argument was reluctantly accepted.

It turned out that the two who had been caught were from the West Riding of Yorkshire and, that the third one who had scampered was from a corner shop about a mile away from the post office and, he lived above the shop with his wife. He had recently been in prison for a "receiving stolen goods" offense and, he had met the other two while he was inside. He'd told them about the dark and dimly lit post office and, they said they had the skills to do the "job" when they got out, so arrangements were made and the "job" was done and, their skills and experience ended up with all three of them being given a five year holiday in the Queen's Hotel at Her Majesties Pleasure.

Despite the procrastinations of the Charge Room Sergeant on the night of the arrest, on the day of the hearing at the Court of Quarter Sessions the Learned Recorder found fit to commend my actions on the night in question, despite leaving the scene unattended and, not taking the two injured to hospital prior to taking them to the police station.

THE MURKY WATERS

Summer had arrived and presented a beautiful day, I was on an afternoon shift and detailed to police the beat which covered the area where two tidal rivers met, where there was a pier and dock gates for entrance to the docks in the middle of the city. When the tide was right the small bridges would be raised and the flood gates opened to allow the vessels through. The water in the rivers and the docks and basins was always muddy and murky, because of the tides drifting the silt and mud in to the dock walls and, dredging was an ever ongoing exercise to keep the gates being able to be opened and closed.

Walking the beat was a pleasure, the sun was shining, the seamen, the warehouse men in the fruit and vegetable markets were as usual always pleasant and, the site seers strolling the river fronts and the dock sides were enjoying the sun.

Five o'clock arrived and it was my time to partake of my packing up in the police box which was situated near to a dock entrance from the major river and, at the side of the Fireboat Office and Launch Pad. The box had windows on both sides, it was equipped with a desk to write your reports on (If you received permission to do so) and, a kettle to make a cup of tea or coffee. The door would also close to give you some privacy, the windows would also open to give you some air and, there was a telephone to lift to be connected to the divisional control room. The down side was that with it being a felt roof, the roof invariably leaked when it rained and there were no toileting facilities - I suppose the designers didn't think that coppers had to spend a penny and, because there weren't any such facilities the then brains of the police force were obviously of the same mind as the designers.

On going into the box for the three quarters of an hour break I opened the windows, took my tunic and helmet off, wiped the sweat from my brow caused by the heat of the day and undid my detached collar and tie - what a relief. With it being lovely weather and dry my packing up was also dry - what a relief. If I wanted to go to the toilet then I would have to re-adjust my collar and tie, put on my tunic and helmet and visit the Fireboat Office, because on leaving the box and placing myself into the outside elements and scene I had to be fully kitted out . If I wasn't there was the risk of a visit from the Duty Sergeant and, facing a charge of being improperly dressed.

I'd enjoyed my sandwiches and cup of tea and, I was nearing the end of my break, when nature took control, so I re-adjusted my dress and, was just about to open the door to visit the fireboat office for a leak, when I heard one hell of a crash. I looked out of the window and, saw that the tractor of an articulated lorry had hit the bridge side on the lock gate and gone over into the dock entrance . I could see the lorry slowly sinking into the water.

Reflex action took over and, I opened the door of the police box and ran the twenty yards or so to the scene, at the same time discarding my helmet, tunic, collar and tie, which I'd just put back on to visit the firemen's loo. I totally forgot about the loo, as I looked at the vehicle I could see half of the passenger side window of the vehicle and a red headed person struggling to get to it. The cab was going down fast, so there was only one thing to do and, that was to get in there and somehow break the window and give him a chance to get out..

I jumped in and straight away I was on the side of the cab trying to kick at the part of the passenger window that was still above the water level. No-matter how hard I was able to kick, the glass wouldn't break. The vehicle was sinking fast, I went under with it, the mud was disturbed even worse, the suck of the water was increasing and I was going down with it, there was nothing else to do but to get out if I could.

I surrendered to the elements and fought to the side, after having taken in copious mouthfuls of the drink that was a mixture of the river mixed with silt and oil, getting back to a breathing position

131

was just an experience of being able to say , "bloody hell, I'm still alive!". That obviously didn't assist the poor person who was trapped in the cab of the vehicle.

By the time I surfaced there was help on the side of the dock and, I was hauled out coughing and spluttering but, that poor driver was still in the cab dieing, nothing further could be done for him, sadly he died.

Needless to say I was soaked, I was sad at the inevitable death of the driver and, I'd then got a sudden death on my hands to report to the Coroner, as the Coroner's Officer.

The vehicle eventually was lifted from the dock gates and, the driver recovered. His family informed and, he was given the send off that his family wanted, with a thanks to me for diving into the murky waters.

I'd now been in the City for some nine months, my extended probationary period had expired and, on the exact date of the finish of my Probationary Period I was transferred to the C.I.D. What a relief! They wanted me there, despite me being Welsh, despite me being questionably arrogant, but they seemed to respect the positive truth of my duty performed.

It was a sad ending for the lorry driver and, I felt for him and his family, but it was an incident that couldn't be rectified by the return of his life.

My extra nine month Probationary Period as a police officer was now over and, my future was before me, the rest is more than another book in itself, "THAT'S HOW IT ALL STARTED".